A NEW YORK TIMES COMPANY PUBLICATION

Family Circle's Great Desserts

EDITOR: NANCY HECHT FITZPATRICK
ART DIRECTOR: MARSHA J. CAMERA
ART ASSOCIATE: WALTER C. SCHWARTZ
PRODUCTION MANAGER: NORMAN ELLERS

Cover photograph by George Nordhausen
Recipe for Peach Melba Bavarian shown on cover is on page 109.

All recipes tested in Family Circle's Test Kitchens

Contents

Right: Cherries Jubilee is a heavenly ice cream creation that takes only minutes to make. The recipe is on page 94.

Introduction: It's A Great Dessert

When it's sumptuous but simple-to-make, it's a great dessert. When it's luscious but low-calorie, it's a great dessert. When it's classic but convenient, it's a great dessert. Of course, a great dessert can also be something to idly take pleasure in creating—a cream puff or torte that takes time but offers "I made it myself" satisfaction. This book is dedicated to all these things and more. It offers over 200 recipes for all kinds of desserts including cakes, cookies, pies and ice cream. Some of the recipes are brand new creations, others are classical in origin. But all are designed to make dessert a beautiful, delicious, spectacular experience. We've added drawings, also, to help when it comes time to decorate cakes, cookies and pies, to make gelatin desserts and fruit garnishes. There are even directions for making your own pastry bag. In this section we've added a few other extras, too, such as the equivalents chart below. All in all, the idea is to give you a collection of recipes you can call on any day you want a great dessert. How about today?

Quick And Easy Dessert Chart

FOOD	EQUIVALENTS
Dairy:	
Whole eggs, 1 cup	About 6 large
Egg yolks, 1 cup	11 to 12
Egg whites, 1 cup	7 to 8
1 whole egg	2 egg yolks
Cheddar and Swiss cheese, 1 pound	4 cups shredded
Parmesan cheese, grated, 3 ounces	1 cup
Milk, skim, 1 cup	$^1/_3$ cup instant non-fat dry milk plus 1 cup minus 1 tablespoon water
Milk, sweetened condensed (14$^1/_2$ ounces)	1$^2/_3$ cups
Milk, evaporated, tall can	1$^2/_3$ cups
Milk, evaporated, small can	$^2/_3$ cup
Butter or margarine, 1 pound	4 sticks, 2 cups
Butter or margarine, whipped, 1 pound	3 cups
Butter or margarine, 4 Tbs.	$^1/_2$ stick, $^1/_4$ cup
Buttermilk or soured milk, 1 cup	1 tablespoon vinegar plus sweet milk to equal 1 cup
Heavy cream, 1 cup	2 cups whipped
Ice Cream, $^1/_2$ gallon	4 pints

FOOD	EQUIVALENTS
Fruit:	
Apples, 1 pound	3 cups, sliced
Lemon, 1 medium	2 tsps. grated rind, and 2 Tbs. juice

FOOD	EQUIVALENTS
Orange, 1 medium	4 tsps. grated rind, and $^1/_3$ cup juice
Nuts:	
Almonds, shelled, 1 pound	3$^1/_2$ cups
Peanuts, shelled, 1 pound	3 cups
Pecans, shelled, 1 pound	4 cups
Walnuts, shelled, 1 pound	4 cups
Starches and Sugars:	
Rice, regular, $^1/_2$ cup	2 cups cooked
Graham crackers, 11 squares	1 cup crumbs
Bread, fresh, 1 slice	$^1/_2$ cup crumbs
Sugar, granulated, 1 pound	2 cups
Sugar, brown, 1 pound	2$^1/_4$ cups (packed)
Sugar 10X, 1 pound	About 4 cups
Flour, all-purpose, 1 pound	4 cups, sifted
Corn syrup, 1 cup	1 cup sugar, plus $^1/_4$ cup liquid
Cornstarch (to thicken), 1$^1/_2$ teaspoons	1 tablespoon flour
Tapioca (to thicken), 2 teaspoons	1 tablespoon flour
Miscellaneous:	
Baking powder, 1 teaspoon	$^1/_4$ tsp. baking soda plus $^5/_8$ tsp. cream of tartar
Chocolate, unsweetened, 1 square	3 Tbs. cocoa plus 1 Tbs. fat

Left: Cherry Cordial Chocolate Soufflé is a romantically beautiful dessert that's easy to make. See Chapter 8 for the recipe.

Fruit Garnishes Are Easy To Make

Fruit offers one of the easiest, quickest ways to decorate just about any dessert, as we show you here. Try these garnish ideas on your next pudding, pie, cake or ice cream creation.

To Store Berries: Empty them from their carton, then place (without washing or hulling) in a single layer in a shallow pan. This makes it easy to spot any soft ones to set aside for eating right away. Cover pan lightly and chill. To enjoy them at their best, hold no more than a day.

To Wash: Leave hulls on to save the juice, then place the berries in a strainer or colander and let a gentle spray of cool water run over them. Or if they seem extra sandy, swish the strainer up and down in a pan of water, changing it several times, then drain.

To Hull: Take your choice of "tools"—your fingers, a knife or a teaspoon. When the berry is ripe, the hull will pull out easily with a gentle twist. Since juices do stain, you may wish to use a knife tip or scoop out each hull with a spoon.

To Make a Double-Berry Cup: Make cuts lengthwise from tip almost to stem in a large berry; spread "petals." Place whole berry, tip up, in center.

To Make Rosettes: Slice berries lengthwise, then outline a circle in center of dessert with some of the largest slices, points out. Continue with overlapping circles to center; using smallest slices last. Finish with a whole berry.

To Make a Snowdrop: Dip berry into 10X (confectioners') sugar to coat generously, leaving the hull on for a handle. This is the easiest, fastest way to make a pretty garnish for puddings, pies and cheesecakes.

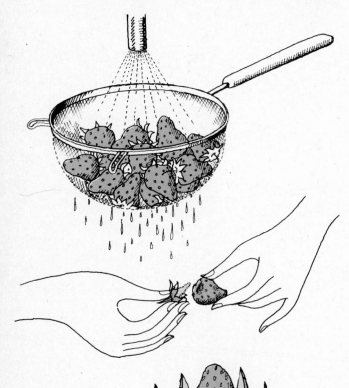

HOW TO STORE CAKES AND COOKIES

Bake your cakes when you have the creative urge and then store or freeze them for later serving. Be sure your cakes are completely cooled before storing or freezing.

To store cakes: Cover any cut surfaces with wax paper to keep moist. Cakes can be stored in a cake keeper or with a large bowl inverted over cake on serving plate for several days. Unfrosted cakes freeze best and will store in freezer for up to 4 months. Simply wrap cakes in aluminum foil, transparent wrap, or in plastic bags and freeze. They will thaw in about 1 hour at room temperature. Frosted cakes, too, can be frozen but they should be frozen on a piece of cardboard or a cooky sheet until firm, then wrapped in aluminum foil, transparent wrap, or very large plastic bags. They will keep about 3 months. Thaw at room temperature for 2 hours.

Storing Fruitcakes: Fruitcakes mellow and improve with time. If you want to make your cake ahead and keep it for the holidays, here's how: Sprinkle cake with brandy or rum, if you wish. Wrap cake securely in heavy foil. Cakes may be kept at room temperature at least one week; in the refrigerator, 1 month; or in the freezer, 3 months. Glaze and garnish cake the day you wish to use it.

Cookies: Place soft cookies in a canister or box with a tight cover to keep moisture in. Short on containers? Seal cookies in a transparent bag and tuck away in the cupboard. To keep crisp cookies crisp, or fancy cut-outs from breaking, layer with transparent wrap, foil or wax paper between in a large shallow pan or roaster or on a tray. Bar cookies can stay right in their baking pan tightly covered with foil.

Note: For storing pies and other desserts, follow the tips given with specific recipes.

THE RIGHT INGREDIENTS

1. Cake flour is used in all recipes.
2. Shortening: Soft shortening, as called for in some recipes, is found in one- and three-pound cans.
3. Vegetable oil is used only in chiffon cakes.
4. Butter or margarine (not whipped or diet) comes in the handy stick form.
5. Baking powder: Double-action is used in all recipes.

WHEN CAKE IS DONE

The best of ovens sometimes vary in temperature. Therefore, you need some way of knowing when your cake is done. Here are three ways:
1. Follow time given in recipe plus your judgment.
2. Notice that baked cake shrinks slightly from sides of pan. (Not foam cakes.)
3. Touch center of cake lightly with fingertip. If baked, the top will spring back to shape; if not baked, imprint will remain.

HOW TO COOL CAKES

Cool foam cakes upside down over bottle until cold. (Don't worry, the cake won't fall out.) This keeps your cake high and light until the delicate walls are cool enough to support the weight of the cake.

Cool butter cakes on wire racks to allow air to circulate around hot cake.

MAKE YOUR OWN PASTRY BAG

No pastry bag? Make one this way: Tear off a 12-inch square of waxed paper, fold it into a triangle and cut in half. Holding corners B and C of long side, curl toward A as shown, pulling tightly until all three points meet. (Point at bottom should be closed.) Fill cone with frosting; snip off point to whatever size opening you wish.

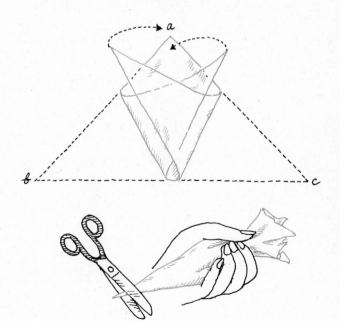

BAKING TERMS

Bake	To cook by dry heat, usually in an oven
Batter	A mixture of flour and liquid plus other ingredients, such as sugar, thin enough to drop or pour
Beat	To make a mixture smooth or to introduce air by using a brisk, regular over-and-over motion
Blend	To mix two or more ingredients together thoroughly
Boil	To cook a liquid or in a liquid in which bubbles break on surface (212° F at sea level)
Caramelize	To heat sugar slowly until it becomes brown in color and caramel in flavor
Chop	To cut food into fine pieces with knife or mechanical chopper
Cream	To blend two or more foods until smooth and fluffy
Cut	To combine shortening or liquid with dry ingredients using pastry blender or two knives
Dissolve	To make a solution from a dry and a liquid ingredient
Fold	To combine ingredients using an up-over-and-down motion
Scald	To heat liquid to just below boiling point
Sift	To put dry ingredients through a sieve
Simmer	To cook a liquid or in a liquid at a temperature just below boiling. Bubbles form slowly and break just below the surface
Stir	To mix using circular motion
Whip	To beat rapidly to incorporate air and increase volume

EQUIVALENT MEASURES

1½ teaspoons	= ½ tablespoon
3 teaspoons	= 1 tablespoon
2 tablespoons	= 1 ounce
4 tablespoons	= ¼ cup
5 tablespoons plus 1 teaspoon	= ⅓ cup
8 tablespoons	= ½ cup
10 tablespoons plus 2 teaspoons	= ⅔ cup
12 tablespoons	= ¾ cup
16 tablespoons	= 1 cup (8 ounces)
2 cups	= 1 pint
2 pints	= 1 quart
4 quarts	= 1 gallon

BAKING AT HIGH ALTITUDES

Most sea-level cake recipes need no modifications up to altitudes of 3,000 feet. Above that, these slight adjustments* are often necessary:

- Usually a *decrease* in leavening or sugar (or both), and an *increase* in liquid are needed.
- Rich butter or shortening cakes may require a *decrease* in shortening by 1 or 2 tablespoons.
- Angel food, chiffon, or sponge cakes may require an *increase* in eggs. They should be slightly underbeaten, since overbeating will result in a dry cake.
- If recipe calls for baking soda, try a slight *decrease* in amount.

*Each of these adjustments may be required to a greater or lesser degree, according to the type of cake being prepared and the proportion of ingredients to each other. Use the table below as a starting point or guide.

Altitude	3,000 to 4,000 feet	4,000 to 6,000 feet	6,000 to 7,500 feet
Reduce Baking Powder For each teaspoon, decrease	⅛ tsp.	⅛ to ¼ tsp.	¼ tsp.
Reduce Sugar For each cup, decrease	1 Tbs.	1 to 2 Tbs.	3 to 4 Tbs.
Increase liquid For each cup, add	1 to 2 Tbs.	2 to 4 Tbs.	3 to 4 Tbs.
Baking Temperature	Increase 25°	Increase 25°	Increase 25°

Note: When two amounts are given, try the smaller adjustment first; then if cake still needs improvement, use the larger adjustment the next time you make the cake.

There's good reason why cake is one of the very first things any cook learns to create. What could be more popular, easier to make and, at the same time, endless in its flavor possibilities? Made from scratch or from a mix, it takes well to frosting or to a simple sprinkling of sugar on top. It offers a sweet ending to a meal or a not-too-sweet taste treat in mid-afternoon. Consider all these things and you'll realize that one chapter of recipes is just not enough to do justice to this favorite. That's why we've added more cake recipes in our low-calorie and Big Moment Desserts chapters. Plus this chapter includes illustrated decorating tips we hope you'll use to make all your cakes super-sumptuous!

KINDS OF PANS

Cake pans are made in standard sizes, and most are marked by size on the bottom. You may substitute one size for the other in most cakes (see chart below). However, the baking time may vary slightly. The most popular cake pans used are those shown here.

Round—8 and 9 inch
Square—8 and 9 inch
Bundt tube pan—9 inch
Angel cake tube pan—9 and 10 inch
Oblong—13x9x2 inch
Loaf—9x5x3 inch

To be sure your cake pans are the diameter and depth called for in a recipe, measure them with a ruler.

ALTERNATE PAN CHART

If Your Recipe Calls For:	You May Use:
Three 8x1½-inch round pans	Two 9x9x2-inch square pans
Two 9x1½-inch round pans	Two 8x8x2-inch square pans OR: One 13x9x2-inch oblong pan
One 9x5x3-inch loaf pan	One 9x9x2-inch square pan

PREPARING PANS

Use a generous coating of vegetable shortening (unless otherwise specified) and a light dusting of flour for an even, golden crust. For foam cakes, pans are never greased, since the airy cake batter needs to cling to the sides of the pan as it expands.

WHERE TO PUT PANS IN OVEN

When baking one layer or an oblong, place in center of rack.

When baking two layers, use two racks in center third of oven, layers in opposite corners.

When baking three or four layers, use two racks in center third of oven. Stagger pans in opposite corners of both racks so they do not block heat circulation in oven.

For a tube cake, lower rack to bottom third of oven. Place pan in center.

Left: Banana-Nut Cake topped with Rum Butter Cream Frosting. Recipe is on page 31.

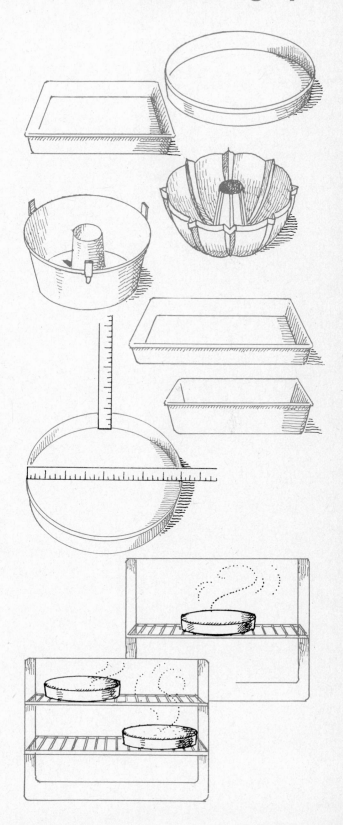

FROSTING THE CAKE

An easy way to frost a cake is to put the cake plate on something you can turn. Place cake plate on a large bowl or sugar canister, then turn as you frost. Of course, if you have a lazy Susan, that is even better. Now ready to frost.

1. First, brush off all the loose crumbs.
2. For layer cakes, frost cakes with flat (bottom) sides together. Cake will be even and steady.
3. Frost entire outside of assembled cake with a very thin layer of frosting and let it set about 20 minutes. The thin coating holds crumbs in place and keeps them from mixing with the final frosting.
4. Frost sides of cake first, then frost top, swirling frosting for that grand finale.

Cake Making Tips That Save You Time

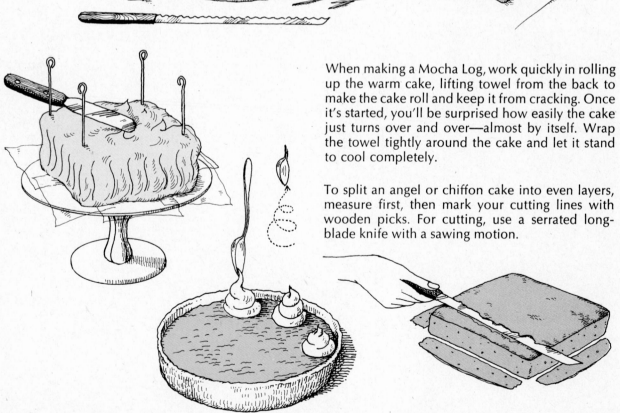

When making a Mocha Log, work quickly in rolling up the warm cake, lifting towel from the back to make the cake roll and keep it from cracking. Once it's started, you'll be surprised how easily the cake just turns over and over—almost by itself. Wrap the towel tightly around the cake and let it stand to cool completely.

To split an angel or chiffon cake into even layers, measure first, then mark your cutting lines with wooden picks. For cutting, use a serrated long-blade knife with a sawing motion.

Have trouble with layers scooting apart after they're filled? Just anchor them in place with long thin metal skewers, and when top of cake is finished, take them out and smooth frosting.

Meringue rosettes are easy-to-make with a teaspoon if you don't have a pastry bag. Spoon up a bit of meringue, then drop into place, swirling upward to a peak.

If a layer humps a bit in the center, shave off flat with a sharp knife. Brush any loose crumbs from edge with a pastry brush so they won't muss frosting; or, trim a thin slice from edges.

Cakes Are Easy To Decorate

Make a Feather Top: Frost cake and drizzle melted chocolate (melt 2 squares with ½ teaspoon shortening) across frosting, in lines about 1 inch apart. Draw edge of spatula across lines.

Spoon Trick: Push the tip of a teaspoon lightly into soft frosting, as shown in drawing. Withdraw spoon quickly to keep lines sharp; repeat, keeping spoon marks in straight line.

Plaid Design: Use a table fork to make a plaid effect on frosting. Pull fork toward you in parallel lines, equally spaced. Turn cake and make lines at right angles to these.

Crisscross Pattern: Draw parallel lines in frosting, about 1 inch apart, using a knife or spatula. Turn cake and draw lines at right angles to first series.

Shadow Design: Drip melted chocolate (prepared as for feather design) from a teaspoon around edge of frosted cake; let chocolate run down sides.

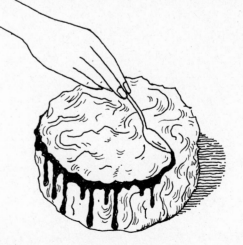

FOAM CAKES

COFFEE CHIFFON CAKE

Bake at 325° for 1 hour and 10 minutes.
Makes one 10-inch tube cake.

2⅓ cups sifted cake flour
1⅓ cups sugar
  3 teaspoons baking powder
  ½ teaspoon salt
  ½ cup vegetable oil
  5 egg yolks
  ¾ cup cold water
  1 tablespoon instant coffee powder
  1 cup (7 to 8) egg whites
  ½ teaspoon cream of tartar
     Mocha Glaze (recipe follows)

1. Sift flour, 1 cup of the sugar, baking powder and salt into a medium-size bowl. Make a well and add in order: Oil, egg yolks, water and coffee; beat with a spoon until smooth.
2. Beat egg whites and cream of tartar in large bowl with electric mixer until foamy-white and double in volume. Beat in remaining ⅓ cup sugar, 1 tablespoon at a time, until meringue stands in firm peaks.
3. Gradually pour egg yolk mixture over beaten whites, gently folding in until no streaks of white remain. Spoon into ungreased 10-inch tube pan.
4. Bake in slow oven (325°) 1 hour and 10 minutes, or until top springs back when lightly pressed with fingertip.
5. Invert pan, placing tube over a quart-size soft-drink bottle; let cake cool completely. When cool, loosen cake around outside edge and tube and down sides with a spatula. Cover pan with serving plate; turn upside down; shake gently; lift off pan. Drizzle Mocha Glaze over top of cake, letting it run down the side.

MOCHA GLAZE

Makes enough for top of one 10-inch tube cake.

  2 tablespoons butter or margarine
  2 squares (1 ounce each) unsweetened chocolate
  1 teaspoon instant coffee powder
  ⅛ teaspoon ground cinnamon
  1 cup sifted 10X (confectioners') sugar
  2 tablespoons hot water

1. Melt butter with chocolate in a small heavy saucepan over very low heat; stir until blended.
2. Remove mixture from heat; stir in coffee and the cinnamon.
3. Add sugar alternately with hot water, beating until smooth.

OLD-FASHIONED SPONGE CAKE

Bake at 325° for 1 hour.
Makes one 9-inch tube cake.

  1 cup sifted cake flour
  1 teaspoon baking powder
  ½ teaspoon salt
  6 eggs, separated
  1 cup sugar
  1 teaspoon grated orange rind

1. Sift flour, baking powder and salt onto wax paper; reserve.
2. Beat egg whites in large bowl with electric mixer at high speed until foamy-white and double in volume. Beat in ½ cup of the sugar, 1 tablespoon at a time, until meringue stands in soft peaks.
3. Beat egg yolks in small bowl at high speed until thick and lemon-color. Beat in remaining ½ cup of the sugar, 1 tablespoon at a time, until mixture is very thick and fluffy. Beat in orange rind.
4. Fold flour mixture, ⅓ at a time, into egg yolk mixture with a wire whip or rubber scraper until completely blended.
5. Fold flour-egg-yolk mixture into meringue until no streaks of white or yellow remain. Pour into an ungreased 9-inch tube pan.
6. Bake in slow oven (325°) 1 hour, or until top springs back when lightly pressed with your fingertip.
7. Invert pan, placing tube over a quart-size soft-drink bottle; let cake cool completely. Loosen cake around the edge and the tube and down the sides with a spatula.
8. Cover pan with a serving plate; shake gently; turn upside down; lift off pan. Sift 10X sugar over top, if you wish; slice and serve the sponge cake with sweetened fresh fruit.

Right: Rich, fudgy Chocolate Nut Upside-Down Cake is paired with a smooth caramel nut topping. Serve warm with whipped cream. Recipe is in this chapter.

PETALED DAFFODIL CAKE

Bake at 325° for 1 hour.
Makes 1 ten-inch round cake.

10 eggs
1 teaspoon cream of tartar
½ teaspoon salt
1⅓ cups granulated sugar
1 teaspoon vanilla
1 cup sifted cake flour
½ teaspoon grated lemon rind
1 cup heavy cream
¼ cup 10X (confectioners') sugar
Yellow food coloring

1. Separate eggs, placing whites in a large bowl, and 4 of the yolks in a medium-size bowl. (Chill remaining 6 yolks in a covered jar to add to scrambled eggs.)
2. Add cream of tartar and salt to egg whites; beat with electric mixer until foamy-white and double in volume. Beat in granulated sugar, 1 tablespoon at a time, beating all the time until sugar dissolves and meringue forms soft peaks; beat in vanilla.
3. Sift flour, ¼ at a time, over top and gently fold in.
4. Add lemon rind to the 4 yolks in bowl; beat until thick. Spoon half of the white batter on top and fold in until no streaks of white remain.
5. Spoon batters by tablespoonfuls, alternating colors, into a 10-inch angel-cake pan. (Do not stir batters in pan.)
6. Bake in slow oven (325°) 1 hour, or until golden and top springs back when lightly pressed with fingertip.
7. Hang cake in pan upside down over a soda-pop bottle; cool completely. Loosen cake around edge and tube with a knife; invert onto a large serving plate.
8. Combine cream with 10X sugar and a few drops food coloring in a medium-size bowl; beat until stiff.
9. Spread part over side and top of cake to make a thin smooth layer. Next, take up spoonfuls of frosting on the back of a teaspoon and press onto cake in rows to make petal shapes. Start at the bottom of cake and make one row all the way around, then continue on up to edge. Finish top the same way, working from outside edge toward center. Chill cake until serving time. Cut in wedges to serve.

CHOCOLATE-CHERRY ROLL

Bake at 400° for 10 minutes.
Makes 8 servings.

4 eggs
1 teaspoon vanilla
¾ cup sugar
½ cup sifted cake flour
⅓ cup unsweetened cocoa powder
1 teaspoon baking powder
½ teaspoon salt
1 quart cherry ice cream
Chocolate Whipped Cream (recipe follows)

1. Butter a 15x10x1-inch baking pan; line with wax paper; butter paper.
2. Beat eggs with vanilla until fluffy-thick and lemon colored in large bowl with electric mixer at high speed. Gradually beat in sugar until mixture is very thick.
3. Sift flour, cocoa powder, baking powder and salt over bowl. Fold in until well-blended. Spread the mixed batter evenly in prepared baking pan.
4. Bake in hot oven (400°) 10 minutes, or until top springs back when lightly touched with fingertip.
5. Loosen cake around edges of pan with a sharp knife. Invert pan onto a clean towel lightly dusted with 10X (confectioners') sugar; peel off wax paper. Cut off edges of cake if they are too crisp to roll.
6. Starting at one end, roll up cake, jelly-roll fashion; wrap in towel. Cool cake completely on a wire rack.
7. Soften ice cream slightly. Unroll cooled cake carefully; spread evenly with softened ice cream; reroll. Place on a cooky sheet. Freeze at least 1 hour.
8. Frost roll with Chocolate Whipped Cream. Freeze until serving time. Cut into 8 thick slices.

CHOCOLATE WHIPPED CREAM

1 cup heavy cream
3 tablespoons instant cocoa mix (with sugar)

Beat cream and cocoa in a small bowl until stiff. Spread on filled Chocolate-Cherry Roll at once. Freeze until ready to serve at dessert time.

Left: Orange Walnut Cake. Add a few extra ingredients to a packaged mix and you're done. The recipe for this dessert is in this chapter.

MADE FROM MIXES

ORANGE WALNUT CAKE

Bake at 350° for 50 minutes.
Makes 1 eight-inch round cake.

   1 package yellow cake mix
   2 eggs
   2 teaspoons grated orange rind
   ½ cup orange juice
   ¾ cup water
   ½ cup finely chopped walnuts
      Orange Glaze (recipe follows)

1. Grease an 8-inch springform pan; flour lightly, tapping out any excess.
2. Combine cake mix, 2 eggs, orange rind and juice, and water in a large bowl; beat, following label directions; stir in walnuts. Pour into prepared pan.
3. Bake in moderate oven (350°) 50 minutes, or until top springs back when lightly pressed with fingertip. Cool in pan on a wire rack 10 minutes. Loosen cake around edge with a knife; release spring and carefully lift off side of pan. Place cake on a wire rack; cool completely. Remove cake from base; place on a serving plate.
4. Make Orange Glaze. Spoon over top of cake, letting mixture drizzle down side. Sprinkle thin strips of orange rind over top.

ORANGE GLAZE: Blend 1 cup sifted 10X (confectioners' powdered) sugar and 1 tablespoon orange juice until smooth in a small bowl; stir in 1 tablespoon more orange juice, part at a time, until glaze is thin enough to pour.

MOCHA TUNNEL CAKE

Makes 8 servings.

   1 package white angel-cake mix
      Water
   1 pint chocolate ice cream
   2 pints coffee ice cream
      Toasted slivered almonds

1. Prepare angel-cake mix with water, bake in a 10-inch angel-cake pan, cool, and remove from pan, following label directions on the mix.

2. Hollow out cake this way: Cut a deep circle around top of cake about ¾ inch in from edge, then cut a second circle about ¾ inch from center hole. Cut ring into large sections and lift out, loosening at bottom with a fork. Place shell on a cooky sheet.
3. Spoon chocolate ice cream, a little at a time, into hollow in cake; cut small slices from ring and fit over ice cream to make a smooth top. (Wrap remaining pieces of cake and set aside for nibbles.) Place cake in freezer while preparing "frosting."
4. Beat coffee ice cream in a large bowl just until soft enough to spread; frost cake all over; sprinkle with almonds. (Work quickly so ice cream doesn't melt.)
5. Freeze at least four hours, or overnight. When ready to serve, place on a serving plate; cut into wedges.

ALMOND FRUIT BASKET

Bake at 350° for 45 minutes.
Makes 1 ten-inch round cake.

   1 package angel-cake mix
      Water
   1 can (about 14 ounces) frozen pineapple, thawed and drained
   1 package (about 12 ounces) frozen peaches, thawed and drained
   2 tablespoons rum or brandy
   ⅔ cup apricot preserves
   ¾ cup sliced almonds, toasted
   4 bananas

1. Prepare cake mix with water, following label directions; pour batter into a 10-inch angel-cake pan.
2. Bake in moderate oven (350°) 45 minutes, or until a long wooden skewer inserted near center comes out clean.
3. Hang cake in pan upside down over a soda-pop bottle; cool completely. Loosen the cake around edge and tube with a knife; invert onto a large serving plate.
4. Combine pineapple, peaches and rum or brandy in a medium-size bowl; toss lightly. Chill at least an hour to blend flavors.
5. Starting ½ inch in from outer edge of cake, cut a coneshape piece from center, using a sharp knife and a sawing motion; lift out and wrap the piece to serve for another dessert.

6. Heat preserves just until bubbly in a small saucepan; press through a sieve into a small bowl. Brush over outside of cake to glaze evenly; press almonds into glaze.

7. Just before serving, peel bananas and slice; add to chilled fruits; spoon into hollow in cake. Garnish with maraschino cherries, if you wish. Cut cake in wedges, serving some of the fruit with each piece.

ORANGE SUNBURST

Makes 1 ten-inch round cake.

1 package orange chiffon-cake mix
Eggs
Water
½ cup sugar
¼ cup light rum
¾ cup orange marmalade
Fluffy Orange Frosting (recipe follows)
½ cup chopped pistachio nuts
2 seedless oranges, pared, sectioned and drained

1. Prepare cake mix with eggs and water, bake in a 10-inch angel-cake pan, cool and remove from pan, following label directions. Split cake horizontally; lift off top layer; turn cut edge up.

2. Combine sugar and ½ cup water in a small saucepan. Heat, stirring constantly, to boiling, then simmer 2 minutes; cool slightly; stir in rum. Spoon over cake layers.

3. Spread ½ cup of the orange marmalade over bottom layer; place on a serving plate. Top with remaining layer, cut side down.

4. Prepare Fluffy Orange Frosting; spread over side and top, making deep swirls with spatula.

5. Heat remaining ¼ cup orange marmalade until melted in a small saucepan; place pistachio nuts on wax paper. Dip one end of each orange section into marmalade, then into pistachio nuts. Arrange on top of cake. Cut in wedges.

FLUFFY ORANGE FROSTING: In the top of a large double boiler, combine 2 unbeaten egg whites, 1¼ cups sugar, 1 tablespoon light corn syrup and ¼ cup thawed frozen concentrate for orange juice; place top over simmering water. Cook, beating constantly with an electric beater at high speed, 10 minutes, or until frosting stands in firm peaks; remove from heat.

TOASTED ALMOND BUTTER TORTE

Bake at 350° for 35 minutes.
Makes 1 nine-inch cake.

1 package yellow cake mix
Eggs
Water
1 package (6 ounces) sliced almonds
1 package creamy fudge frosting mix
½ cup (1 stick) butter or margarine
1 tablespoon instant coffee
1 package creamy vanilla frosting mix
1½ cups sifted 10X (confectioners') sugar

1. Prepare cake mix with eggs and water; bake in two 9x1½-inch layer cake pans. Cool, and remove from pans, following label directions.

2. While cake bakes, spread almonds in a shallow pan; heat in same oven 12 minutes, or until lightly toasted; set aside.

3. Prepare fudge frosting mix with ¼ cup of the butter or margarine and warm water, following label directions.

4. Dissolve instant coffee in ¼ cup warm water in a medium-size bowl; add vanilla frosting mix and remaining ¼ cup butter or margarine; prepare, following label directions; stir in 10X sugar until smooth. Put cake layers together with coffee frosting. Place on a serving plate. Spread chocolate frosting on side and top of cake; sprinkle all over with reserved toasted almonds. Slice and serve.

CHIFFON CAKE TOWER

Makes 8 to 10 servings.

1 eight- or nine-inch packaged chiffon cake
1 can (5 ounces) vanilla pudding
1 jar (10 ounces) cherry preserves
1 package vanilla glaze mix

1. Split cake into 4 layers. Place first layer on serving plate; spread with ⅓ of pudding, then spread about 4 tablespoons of preserves over pudding. Top with next layer. Repeat with remaining pudding, preserves and cake, ending with cake.

2. Prepare glaze, following label directions. Spread on top of cake, letting it drizzle down the side of cake. Garnish top with preserves, if you wish; refrigerate until ready to serve.

FRUITCAKES

PLANTATION FRUITCAKE

Bake at 300° for 2 hours.
Makes 1 nine-inch tube cake.

  2 cups seedless raisins
  1 can (1 pound) cling peaches, drained and chopped
  1 cup vegetable shortening
  1 cup firmly packed brown sugar
  ½ cup cream sherry or orange juice
  1 jar (1 pound) mixed candied fruits
  2 cups chopped walnuts
  4 eggs, beaten
2½ cups sifted all-purpose flour
  1 teaspoon baking powder
1½ teaspoons salt
  1 teaspoon ground cinnamon
  ½ teaspoon ground cloves
  ¼ cup light corn syrup

1. Butter a 9-inch bundt pan. Dust with flour; tap out excess.
2. Combine raisins, peaches, shortening, brown sugar and sherry or orange juice in a medium-size saucepan; heat just to boiling. Remove from heat; cool.
3. Add candied fruit and nuts to cooked mixture; stir in beaten eggs.
4. Sift flour, baking powder, salt, cinnamon and cloves onto wax paper; stir into fruit mixture. Spoon into prepared pan.
5. Bake in slow oven (300°) 2 hours, or until center springs back when pressed with fingertip. Cool in pan on wire rack 15 minutes; turn out of pan; cool completely. Heat corn syrup just until bubbly in a small saucepan. Brush syrup over cake.

EASY NOËL FRUITCAKE

Bake at 350° for 1 hour.
Makes 1 medium-size tube cake or 1 loaf cake.

  1 package (17 ounces) apricot nut bread mix
  1 jar (1 pound) mixed candied friuts
  1 cup chopped pecans
  ½ cup seedless raisins
  ½ cup whole blanched almonds (optional)
  ¼ cup light corn syrup

1. Butter a 6-cup fancy tube pan or a 9x5x3-inch loaf pan; line bottom with wax paper; butter paper. (If tube pan is not flat on bottom, butter very well; dust with flour; tap out excess.)
2. Prepare the mix, following label directions, adding fruit, pecans and raisins with dry mix. Turn into pan. Arrange almonds on batter.
3. Bake in moderate oven (350°) 1 hour, or until top springs back when lightly pressed.
4. Cool in pan on wire rack 10 minutes. Turn out of pan; remove wax paper, cool completely.
5. Heat corn syrup just until bubbly in small pan; brush over cake. Decorate with candied cherries, if you wish.

DUBLIN HOLLY CAKE

Bake at 325° for 1 hour, 30 minutes.
Makes 1 ten-inch tube cake.

  1 jar (1 pound) candied mixed fruits
  1 package (11 ounces) currants
1½ cups chopped walnuts
  2 tablespoons grated orange rind
  4 cups sifted all-purpose flour
  2 teaspoons apple-pie spice
  1 teaspoon baking soda
  1 teaspoon salt
  1 cup (2 sticks) butter or margarine
1⅓ cups firmly packed brown sugar
  3 eggs
  1 cup stout or dark ale

1. Butter a 10-inch tube pan; dust with flour; tap out excess.
2. Combine candied fruits, currants, chopped walnuts and orange rind in a very large bowl.
3. Sift flour, apple-pie spice, baking soda and salt onto wax paper. Sprinkle ¼ cup of mixture over fruits and nuts and toss to coat.
4. Beat butter or margarine, brown sugar, eggs in large bowl with electric mixer at high speed, 3 minutes, until fluffy.
5. Stir in remaining flour mixture alternately with stout or ale, beating after each addition.
6. Pour batter over prepared fruit and nuts and fold just until well-blended. Spoon into pan.
7. Bake in slow oven (325°) 1 hour and 30 minutes, or until center springs back when lightly pressed with fingertip. Cool in pan on wire rack for 15 minutes; loosen around edge and tube with a knife; turn out onto wire rack; cool.

Abby's Fabulous Chocolate Cake offers dessert makers a chance to show their creativity—easily and deliciously. The recipe is in this chapter.

Starting at left and moving clockwise: Burnt Sugar-Chocolate Cake, Silk and Satin Chocolate Mousse, Breton Chocolate Pound Cake, Hungarian Chocolate Squares and Black Bottom Pie. See index for recipe page numbers.

CHOCOLATE CURLS

Makes enough curls to decorate a 9-inch cake.

Melt 7 squares semisweet chocolate in a small bowl over hot water, stirring often. Turn out onto cold cooky sheet. Spread out to a 6x4-inch rectangle. Refrigerate just until set. Pull a long metal spatula across chocolate, letting the soft chocolate curl up in front of the spatula. Place curls on wax paper. It takes a little practice, so count on a few to be less than perfect; put these on the cake first. Save prettiest curls for the top.

GOLDEN FRUITCAKE

Bake at 325° for 1 hour and 40 minutes.
Makes 1 ten-inch cake.

    2 packages (1 pound, 1 ounce each)
      poundcake mix
    4 eggs
      Milk or water
    1 jar (8 ounces) candied red cherries,
      chopped
    1 cup whole blanched almonds, chopped
    ½ cup golden raisins, chopped
    ¼ cup cognac
    1 can (3½ ounces) flaked coconut
    2 tablespoons grated orange rind
    1 tablespoon grated lemon rind
      Orange Frosting (recipe follows)

1. Butter a 10-inch angel-cake pan; flour lightly, tapping out any excess.
2. Prepare both packages of poundcake mix with eggs and milk or water, following label directions.
3. Combine cherries, almonds and raisins in a medium-size bowl; stir in cognac. Fold into batter with coconut and orange and lemon rinds. Spoon into prepared pan.
4. Bake in slow oven (325°) 1 hour and 40 minutes, or until top springs back when lightly pressed with fingertip. Cool 10 minutes in pan on a wire rack. Loosen cake around edge and tube with a knife; turn onto rack; turn right side up; cool completely.
5. Make Orange Frosting; spread over top of cake, letting mixture run down side. Decorate with candied cherries, angelica and almonds.

ORANGE FROSTING: Combine 1½ cups sifted 10X (confectioners') sugar, 1 tablespoon cognac and 1 tablespoon orange juice in a small bowl; beat until smooth. Spread over top and side of Golden Fruitcake.

DIAMOND HEAD FRUITCAKE

Bake at 275° for 2 hours.
Makes 2 medium-size fruitcakes.

    3 jars (4 ounces each) candied pineapple,
      chopped
    3 jars (4 ounces each) candied orange peel,
      chopped
    1 can (4 ounces) flaked coconut
 1½ cups golden raisins
    1 cup chopped pecans or macadamia nuts
 2½ cups sifted cake flour
    1 teaspoon baking powder
    ½ teaspoon salt
    ½ cup (1 stick) butter or margarine
    1 cup sugar
    4 eggs
    ½ cup pineapple juice
    ¼ cup light corn syrup
      Red and green candied cherries
      Pecan halves

1. Butter two 8½x4½x2½-inch loaf pans; dust lightly with flour; tap out any excess.
2. Combine fruits and nuts in a large bowl.
3. Sift flour, baking powder and salt onto wax paper. Sprinkle ¼ cup of mixture over fruits and nuts; toss to coat.
4. Beat butter or margarine, sugar and eggs in large bowl with electric mixer at high speed for 3 minutes, until fluffy.
5. Stir in remaining flour mixture alternately with pineapple juice, beating after each addition, until the batter is quite smooth.
6. Pour batter over prepared fruits and nuts and fold just until well-blended. Spoon batter into prepared pans.
7. Bake in very slow oven (275°) for 2 hours, or until centers spring back when lightly pressed with fingertip.
8. Cool cakes in pans on wire rack for 15 minutes; loosen around edges with a knife; turn out onto wire racks; cool completely.
9. To decorate: Heat corn syrup in small saucepan just until bubbly; brush over cakes. Garnish with halved candied cherries and pecan halves.

TORTES AND SPECIALS

MOCHA CHESTNUT TORTE

Bake at 325° for 30 minutes.
Makes 12 servings.

4 eggs, separated
1 cup sugar
¼ cup cold brewed coffee
½ teaspoon vanilla
1 cup sifted cake flour
1½ teaspoons baking powder
¼ teaspoon salt
1 package (6 ounces) semisweet chocolate
pieces
1 can (1 pound) chestnuts
2 egg yolks
2 tablespoons hot brewed coffee
½ teaspoon vanilla
½ cup (1 stick) butter or margarine
3 cups heavy cream
½ cup sifted 10X (confectioners') sugar
½ cup unsweetened cocoa powder
Chocolate Leaves (recipe follows)
Chestnut Filling (recipe follows)
Maraschino cherries

1. Butter bottoms only of 2 nine-inch round layer-cake pans. Line with wax paper; butter paper.
2. Beat egg whites in large bowl of electric mixer until foamy-white. Add ½ cup of the sugar gradually, beating all the time until meringue stands in stiff peaks.
3. Beat egg yolks in small bowl with electric mixer until thick and lemon color; gradually beat in remaining ½ cup sugar until mixture is very thick and light. Stir in cold coffee. Fold yolk mixture gently into meringue until no streaks of white remain.
4. Put flour, baking powder and salt into sifter; sift over egg mixture, a small amount at a time. Fold in gently. Pour into prepared pans.
5. Bake in slow oven (325°) 30 minutes, or until tops spring back when lightly pressed with fingertip.
6. Invert cake pans with their edges resting on the bottom of custard cups (to keep sponge layers high and light); cool. Remove from pans; peel paper. Split each layer into 2 thin layers.
7. Make Chocolate Leaves: Melt semisweet

chocolate in top of a double boiler over simmering water. Spread ½ the chocolate in a thin even layer on foil on a cooky sheet; chill. Cut out leaf shapes for decorating. Reserve remaining chocolate for Chestnut Filling.
8. Make Chestnut Filling: Drain chestnuts, reserving liquid. Reserve 8 whole chestnuts for decoration. Place 2 egg yolks, 3 tablespoons liquid from chestnuts, remaining chestnuts, coffee, remaining melted chocolate and vanilla in container of an electric blender. Whirl until smooth, scraping sides of container once or twice. Blend in small pieces of butter or margarine until smooth. Chill until spreadable.
9. Put cake layers together with Chestnut Filling. Combine 2 cups of the cream, cocoa and ½ cup 10X sugar in a medium-size bowl; beat until stiff. Spread on top and side of cake.
10. Beat remaining 1 cup cream with remaining 1 tablespoon 10X sugar in a small bowl until stiff. Fill a pastry bag fitted with a notched tube; decorate cake as you wish. Garnish with reserved chestnuts, chocolate leaves and maraschino cherries. Refrigerate until serving time. Sift 10X sugar over top, if you wish.

ZUGER KIRSCHTORTE

Makes 12 servings. (See Note on page 25.)

The Sponge Cake:
4 whole eggs
2 egg yolks
¾ cup granulated sugar
½ cup sifted all-purpose flour
6 tablespoons sifted cornstarch
5 tablespoons butter or margarine, melted
and cooled to lukewarm

1. Preheat oven to 350 degrees. Butter a 9-inch cake pan and dust lightly with flour. The cake pan must have at least a 2-inch rim. If it does not, tie on a collar of waxed paper or aluminum foil, buttered or use a 9-inch springform pan.
2. In a large bowl, combine the eggs, egg yolks and sugar and beat at high speed until thick and light yellow. The mixture will triple in volume.
3. Sift together the flour and cornstarch and with a spatula fold into the egg mixture. Add the melted and cooled butter or margarine and mix only until it is completely absorbed.
4. Pour the batter into the cake pan and bake

350° for 25 to 30 minutes, or until golden brown on top and springy to the touch. Cool the cake in the pan for 5 to 10 minutes and unmold onto a sugared square of wax paper.

The Almond Meringue:

- ½ cup egg whites (4 egg whites)
- 1 cup granulated sugar
- ⅓ cup blanched almonds, ground
- ½ tablespoon flour

5. Reduce oven to 275°. Beat whites with ⅓ cup of sugar until they form soft peaks. Gradually add another ⅓ cup sugar until it is absorbed and the egg whites form stiff peaks.
6. Mix together ⅓ cup sugar, ground almonds and flour, and fold into the beaten egg white mixture until thoroughly blended.
7. Using waxed freezer wrap (or baking paper), cut off two square pieces and with a pencil, trace an 8-inch circle on each square. Dust lightly with flour and place each square on a baking sheet. Using a pastry bag with a small tube, cover the circles with meringue. Start with a small dot in the center and continue circling until the drawn circle is completely covered (like a coiled rope). Or use a spatula and spread the meringue ½ inch thick.
8. Bake (275°) for about 30 minutes, or until a light gold color and crisp. Turn off the oven and let the meringues cool in the oven.

Kirsch Syrup:

- ¼ cup sugar
- ½ cup water
- 2 tablespoons kirsch

9. Bring the sugar and water to a boil and then let cool. Add kirsch.

Additional Ingredients:
- Basic Butter Cream (recipe follows) flavored with 1 tablespoon kirsch
- ½ cup blanched, sliced toasted almonds (for decoration)

10. To assemble cake, cut off a paper-thin layer of the brown crust from the top and bottom of the sponge cake. (This permits the syrup to soak into the sponge cake easily.) Brush top, bottom and side of the cake with the kirsch syrup.
11. Cover one meringue with ¼ inch of butter cream. Place the kirsch-soaked sponge cake on top of the meringue. Spread the top of the sponge cake with about another ¼ inch of butter cream. Place the second meringue on top of the butter cream. Spread the rest of the butter cream all around the sides of the cake. Holding the bottom of the cake in one hand, press the toasted almonds around the side of the cake. Lightly sift confectioners' sugar on top of the cake, if you wish.

Basic Butter Cream:

Yield: 2 cups
- 1 cup granulated sugar
- ¾ cup water
- 4 egg yolks
- 1 cup sifted 10X (confectioners') sugar
- ½ pound unsalted butter

In a saucepan, bring the granulated sugar and water to a boil and cook until it reaches 234 degrees on a candy thermometer, or a medium soft-ball stage.

Place egg yolks in a large bowl and stir in confectioners' sugar. Add the hot, boiled sugar mixture in a thin stream and beat at medium speed, until cooled.

In another bowl, whip the butter until creamy, then beat into the egg yolk mixture until well blended and light. (Keep cool, but do not refrigerate until on cake.)

NOTE: There are cakes and there is Zuger Kirschtorte. Whether you're on a diet or not, I doubt if you will be able to resist the flavor of this cake, which is not overly sweet, and a perfect climax to a festive dinner. This is a traditional torte or cake of Switzerland.

The Sponge Cake will absorb a quantity of the Kirsch syrup and not become soggy, just more delicious. This sponge cake may be used for many types of tortes, for birthday cakes or for any festive cake.

The Basic Butter Cream is versatile. You can flavor it with chocolate, mocha or nut. It is the perfect frosting for cakes and petits fours. Just follow the recipe, step by step and be sure that the egg yolk-sugar syrup mixture has cooled completely before you beat in the butter.

STRAWBERRY VACHERIN

Makes 8 servings.

- **4 egg whites**
- **1 cup superfine granulated sugar**
  Dash of salt
- **½ teaspoon vanilla**
- **2 pints raspberry sherbet**
- **2 cups heavy cream**
- **2 tablespoons Creme de Cassis or blackberry-flavored brandy**
- **2 tablespoons raspberry preserves**
  Strawberries in Cassis (recipe follows)

1. Make three 7-inch rounds on brown paper-lined cooky sheet.
2. Beat egg whites and salt in medium-size bowl until foamy-white. Gradually add sugar, 1 table-spoon at a time, beating well after each addition until meringue stands in firm peaks. Stir in vanilla. Divide meringue among prepared rounds and spread to make a smooth and even surface.
3. Bake in very slow oven (275°) 45 minutes; turn off oven and allow meringues to cool in oven. Loosen meringue layers from brown paper with a long spatula.
4. Line an 8-inch layer-cake with foil. Spread sherbet in pan to make a smooth layer. Cover sherbet with foil and freeze at least 2 hours.
5. To assemble: Beat 1 cup heavy cream in a small bowl until softly mounded; add Creme de Cassis or blackberry-flavored brandy and rasp-berry preserves and beat until stiff.
6. Place 1 meringue layer on a small cooky sheet. Remove sherbet from cake pan and place on meringue layer; top sherbet with second meringue layer and cover with flavored whipped cream from Step 5. Top with remaining me-ringue layer.
7. Beat remaining 1 cup heavy cream until stiff in a small bowl. Frost top and side of cake with part of cream. Fill a pastry bag fitted with a notched tip with remaining whipped cream and pipe cream in a pretty pattern on top of cake.
8. Freeze cake until firm; cover with foil or plastic wrap.
9. To serve: Loosen cake around edge of cooky sheet with a long spatula and slide onto serving plate. Garnish with strawberries dipped in Straw-berries In Cassis. Cut into wedges with a sharp knife and serve with a spoonful of Strawberries In Cassis.

STRAWBERRIES IN CASSIS

Makes about 2½ cups.

- **2 cups (1 pint) fresh strawberries**
- **1 package (10 ounces) frozen red raspberries, thawed**
- **3 tablespoons Creme de Cassis or blackberry-flavored brandy**

1. Wash and hull strawberries. Reserve the 6 largest berries for garnish. Halve the remaining strawberries and place in a bowl.
2. Heat raspberries to boiling in a small sauce-pan. Press through a sieve to remove seeds into a medium-size bowl; add halved strawberries and Creme de Cassis or blackberry-flavored brandy and fold sauce over berries to coat even-ly. Chill at least 1 hour to blend flavors.

BUTTER CAKES

RUTH DOVE'S COCONUT POUND CAKE

Bake at 325° for 1 hour and 15 minutes.
Makes two 9x5x3-inch loaves.

- **4 cups sifted cake flour**
- **10 eggs, separated**
- **2 cups (4 sticks) butter or margarine**
- **2 cups sugar**
- **1 tablespoon vanilla**
- **½ cup flaked coconut, chopped**

1. Butter two 9x5x3-inch loaf pans; dust lightly with flour; tap out any excess.
2. Beat egg whites until foamy-white and dou-ble in volume in a medium-size bowl; beat in ¼ cup sugar, 1 tablespoon at a time, until me-ringue stands in firm peaks.
3. Beat butter or margarine, remaining 1¾ cups sugar and egg yolks in large bowl with mixer at high speed for three minutes. Stir in vanilla.
4. Sift in flour, stirring with a spoon or beating with mixer at low speed, just until blended. Fold in meringue; stir in coconut. Pour into pans.
5. Bake in slow oven (325°) 1 hour and 15 minutes, or until centers spring back.
6. Cool cakes in pans on wire racks 10 min-utes. Loosen around edges with knife; turn out onto racks; cool completely before serving.

Right: Strawberry Vacherin, a meringue-sherbet creation that's covered with whipped cream and strawberries dipped in Cassis. Recipe is above.

BURNT SUGAR-CHOCOLATE CAKE

Bake at 350° for 40 minutes.
Makes 3 eight-inch layers.

- 2½ cups sifted cake flour
- ½ cup dry unsweetened cocoa powder
- 2 teaspoons baking soda
- ½ teaspoon salt
- 1 tablespoon vinegar
- 1 cup milk
- 1 cup shortening
- 2 cups sugar
- 2 eggs
- ½ cup hot water
- 1 teaspoon vanilla
- Burnt Sugar Frosting (recipe follows)

1. Butter and flour 3 eight-inch layer-cake pans; tap out excess.
2. Sift flour, cocoa, baking soda and salt onto wax paper; reserve. Stir vinegar into milk to sour in a cup; reserve.
3. Beat shortening, sugar and eggs in a large bowl with mixer at high speed 3 minutes.
4. Stir in dry ingredients alternately with soured milk, beating after each addition until batter is smooth. Stir in hot water and vanilla; pour batter into prepared cake pans.
5. Bake in moderate oven (350°) 40 minutes, or until centers spring back when lightly pressed.
6. Cool layers in pans on wire racks 10 minutes; loosen around edges with a knife; turn out onto wire racks; cool completely.
7. Put layers together with Burnt Sugar Frosting; frost side and top with remaining frosting; drizzle with reserved syrup.

BURNT SUGAR FROSTING

Makes enough to frost 1 eight-inch triple layer cake.

- ¾ cup granulated sugar
- ¾ cup boiling water
- ¾ cup (1½ sticks) butter or margarine
- 2 egg yolks
- 6 cups sifted 10X (confectioners') sugar

1. Spread granulated sugar in a large heavy skillet; heat very slowly until sugar melts and starts to turn deep golden; add water slowly, stirring constantly. Continue heating until melt-ed sugar dissolves completely in water. Boil syrup rapidly two minutes longer; cool.
2. Beat butter or margarine until smooth in a medium-size bowl; add yolks; blend well.
3. Reserve 2 tablespoons of the cooled syrup for decorating cake; add remaining syrup alternately with 10X sugar to butter mixture; beat until smooth and spreadable.

CHOCOLATE NUT UPSIDE-DOWN CAKE

Bake at 350° for 45 minutes.
Makes 10 servings.

- 10 tablespoons butter or margarine
- ¼ cup firmly packed light brown sugar
- ⅔ cup light corn syrup
- ¼ cup heavy cream
- 1 cup broken walnuts
- 1¾ cups sifted cake flour
- 2 teaspoons baking powder
- ¼ teaspoon salt
- 1½ cups granulated sugar
- 2 eggs, separated
- 3 squares unsweetened chocolate, melted
- 1 teaspoon vanilla
- 1 cup milk

1. Melt 4 tablespoons of the butter or margarine in a small saucepan; stir in brown sugar; heat until bubbly. Stir in corn syrup and cream; heat, stirring constantly, just to boiling. Add nuts; pour into a generously-buttered 10-inch (12-cup) bundt pan (mixture will be thin). Let stand while preparing cake batter.
2. Sift flour, powder and salt onto wax paper.
3. Beat remaining butter or margarine until soft in large bowl. Gradually beat in granulated sugar until well combined. Beat in egg yolks, chocolate and vanilla until well combined.
4. Add flour mixture, alternately with milk, beginning and ending with flour. Beat egg whites until stiff in a small bowl; fold into cake batter. Spoon batter evenly over nut mixture in pan.
5. Bake in moderate oven (350°) 45 minutes, or until cake tester inserted in center comes out clean.
6. Loosen cake from edges with a small knife; cover pan with serving plate; invert; shake gently, then lift off pan. Scoop out any nuts and syrup clinging to pan onto cake with a rubber scraper. Serve with whipped cream.

Left, in the foreground and going clockwise: Dublin Holly Cake, Golden Fruitcake, Plantation Fruitcake and Diamond Head Fruitcake. Recipes are in this chapter.

FRESH APPLE CAKE

Bake at 350° for 35 minutes.
Makes 3 eight-inch square layers.

2 ¾ cups sifted cake flour
1 ½ teaspoons apple-pie spice
 1 teaspoon baking powder
 1 teaspoon baking soda
 1 teaspoon salt
 ½ cup soft shortening
1 ¾ cups sugar
 3 eggs
 2 medium-size tart cooking apples, pared, cored and shredded (2 cups)
 1 teaspoon vanilla
 ½ cup milk
 1 cup very finely chopped walnuts
   Vanilla Butter Cream Frosting (recipe follows)

1. Butter bottoms of three 8x8x2-inch cake pans; line pans with wax paper; butter paper.
2. Sift flour, apple-pie spice, baking powder, baking soda and salt onto wax paper; reserve.
3. Beat shortening, sugar and eggs in large bowl with electric mixer at high speed for 3 minutes. By hand, stir in apples and vanilla.
4. Stir in flour mixture alternately with milk, beating after each addition until batter is smooth. Stir in nuts; pour batter into prepared pans.
5. Bake in moderate oven (350°) 35 minutes, or until centers spring back when lightly pressed with fingertip.
6. Cool layers in pans on wire racks 10 minutes; loosen around edges with a knife; turn out onto wire racks; remove wax paper; cool completely.
7. Put layers together with Vanilla Butter Cream Frosting; frost sides and top with remaining frosting; garnish with walnut halves, if you wish.

VANILLA BUTTER CREAM FROSTING

Makes enough to fill and frost 3 eight-inch square layers.

 ¾ cup (1 ½ sticks) butter or margarine
 7 cups sifted 10X (confectioners') sugar (from 2 one-pound packages)
 ¼ cup milk
 2 teaspoons vanilla
 ¼ teaspoon salt

Beat butter or margarine until soft in a medium-size bowl. Beat in 10X sugar, alternately with milk, vanilla and salt until smooth.

BRETON CHOCOLATE POUND CAKE

Bake at 300° for 1 hour and 45 minutes.
Makes 1 nine-inch tube cake.

 5 squares unsweetened chocolate
1 ⅓ cups water
 2 cups sifted all-purpose flour
 2 cups sugar
 1 teaspoon salt
 ½ cup (1 stick) butter or margarine
 3 eggs
 1 teaspoon aromatic bitters
 1 teaspoon vanilla
 2 teaspoons baking powder
   Chocolate Glaze (recipe follows)

1. Combine chocolate and water in a small saucepan. Heat, stirring constantly, until chocolate melts; cool until lukewarm.
2. Sift flour, sugar and salt into large bowl. Cut in butter or margarine with a pastry blender to make a crumbly mixture.
3. Add cooled chocolate mixture. Beat at medium speed with electric mixer for 5 minutes. Chill batter in bowl for at least 1 hour.
4. Return bowl to mixer. Beat at medium speed 1 minute. Add eggs, 1 at a time, beating 1 minute after each addition. Add aromatic bitters and vanilla and beat 2 minutes. Add baking powder and beat 2 minutes more.
5. Pour batter into a buttered 8-cup tube pan which has been lightly dusted with dry cocoa (or a 9x5x3-inch loaf pan).
6. Bake in slow oven (300°) 1 hour and 45 minutes, or until a toothpick inserted in center comes out clean. Cool cake in pan on wire rack 10 minutes; loosen around edges with a knife. Turn cake out of pan on a wire rack and cool completely.
7. Frost with Chocolate Glaze and garnish with sliced almonds, if you wish.
NOTE: The method for making this cake is a little unusual, but the end product is an extraordinary, fine-textured chocolate pound cake. You really have to beat the batter as long as directed to get the results. This cake stays moist for a long time and can easily be frozen.

CHOCOLATE GLAZE

1 package (4 ounces) sweet cooking
  chocolate
1 tablespoon butter or margarine
3 tablespoons water
1 cup 10X (confectioners') sugar
  Dash of salt
1 teaspoon vanilla

Break chocolate into pieces. Heat with butter or margarine and water in a medium-size saucepan, stirring constantly, until chocolate melts. Remove from heat; beat in sugar and salt until smooth; stir in vanilla.

BANANA-NUT CAKE

Bake at 350° for 30 minutes.
Makes 2 nine-inch layers.

2⅓ cups sifted cake flour
2½ teaspoons baking powder
 ½ teaspoon baking soda
 ½ teaspoon salt
 ½ teaspoon ground cinnamon
 1 cup mashed ripe bananas (2 medium-size)
 ½ cup buttermilk
 ½ cup (1 stick) butter or margarine
1¼ cups sugar
 2 eggs
 ¼ teaspoon vanilla
 ¾ cup chopped walnuts
  Rum Butter Cream Frosting (recipe follows)

1. Butter two 9x1½-inch layer-cake pans; dust lightly with flour; tap out any excess.
2. Sift flour, baking powder, baking soda, salt and cinnamon onto wax paper; reserve. Stir buttermilk into bananas in small bowl; reserve.
3. Beat butter or margarine, sugar and eggs in large bowl with electric mixer at high speed 3 minutes.
4. Stir in flour mixture by hand alternately with banana-milk mixture, beating after each addition until batter is smooth. Stir in vanilla and ¼ cup chopped nuts; pour batter into pans.
5. Bake in moderate oven (350°) 30 minutes, or until centers spring back when lightly pressed.
6. Cool layers in pans on wire racks 10 minutes; loosen around edges with a knife; turn out onto wire racks; cool completely.

7. Put layers together with Rum Butter Cream Frosting; frost side and top with remaining frosting. Press remaining ½ cup chopped nuts on sides of cake. Dip banana slices in orange or pineapple juice to keep white; garnish cake.

RUM BUTTER CREAM FROSTING

Makes enough to fill and frost 2 nine-inch layers.

 ⅓ cup butter or margarine
3½ cups sifted 10X (confectioners') sugar
 ¼ cup milk
1½ teaspoons rum extract

1. Beat butter or margarine in a medium-size bowl until soft.
2. Add 10X sugar alternately with rum extract and milk until creamy-smooth.

ABBY'S FABULOUS CHOCOLATE CAKE

Bake at 350° for 40 minutes.
Makes an 8-inch double-layer cake.

 4 squares unsweetened chocolate
 ½ cup (1 stick) butter or margarine (for cake)
 1 cup water
 2 cups sifted cake flour
1¼ teaspoons baking soda
 1 teaspoon salt
 2 eggs
 1 cup (8 ounces) dairy sour cream
 2 cups sugar
1½ teaspoons vanilla
  Fluffy White Frosting (recipe on page 32)
 1 tablespoon butter or margarine (for topping)

1. Butter 2 eight-inch round layer-cake pans; flour lightly, tapping out any excess.
2. Combine 3 squares of the chocolate, the ½ cup butter or margarine, and water in the top of a double boiler; heat over simmering water until chocolate and butter melt; remove; cool.
3. Sift the flour, soda and salt into a large bowl.
4. Beat eggs with sour cream until blended in a medium-size bowl with electric mixer; beat in sugar and vanilla; stir in cooled chocolate mixture. Beat into flour mixture, half at a time, til smooth. (Batter will be thin.) Pour into pans.
5. Bake in moderate oven (350°) 40 minutes,

or until centers spring back when lightly pressed with fingertip. Cool in pans. Loosen around edges with a knife; turn out onto racks.

6. Make Fluffy White Frosting. Put cake layers together with about one quarter of the frosting on a serving plate; spread remainder on side and top, making deep swirls with spatula.

7. Melt remaining 1 square chocolate with the 1 tablespoon butter or margarine in a cup set in hot water; stir until smooth. Drizzle over top of cake, letting mixture drip down side.

FLUFFY WHITE FROSTING

Makes enough to fill and frost an 8-inch double-layer cake.

    2 egg whites
    ¾ cup sugar
    ½ teaspoon cream of tartar
      Dash of salt
    2½ teaspoons cold water
    1 teaspoon vanilla

1. Combine egg whites, sugar, cream of tartar, salt and water in top of double boiler; beat til blended. Place over simmering water.

2. Cook, beating constantly with an electric or rotary beater, until mixture stands in firm peaks. Remove from water; stir in vanilla.

HUNGARIAN CHOCOLATE SQUARES

Bake at 350° for 15 minutes.
Makes 12 servings.

Cake:
    3 squares unsweetened chocolate
    4 eggs, separated
    ½ cup superfine sugar
    ¾ cup (1½ sticks) butter or margarine
    ⅔ cup sifted cake flour
    ¼ teaspoon salt
    1 teaspoon vanilla
Filling:
    10 squares semisweet chocolate (from two 8-ounce packages)
    2 cups heavy cream
    2 tablespoons coffee liqueur
Frosting:
    1 cup superfine sugar
    ½ cup hot coffee

    6 squares semisweet chocolate
    2 tablespoons light corn syrup
    2 tablespoons butter or margarine
    2 tablespoons coffee liqueur

1. To make cake: Melt chocolate in top of a double boiler over hot water; cool to lukewarm.

2. Butter a 15x10x1-inch baking pan; line with wax paper; butter paper.

3. Beat egg whites until foamy-white and double in volume in a medium-size bowl. Beat in ¼ cup of the sugar, 1 tablespoon at a time, until meringue stands in soft peaks.

4. Beat butter or margarine in a large bowl; gradually add remaining ¼ cup sugar and continue beating until mixture is well-blended. Beat in egg yolks until smooth, then cooled chocolate. Sift flour and salt into chocolate mixture; stir to blend; add vanilla.

5. Stir ⅓ of the meringue mixture from Step 3 into chocolate mixture; fold in remaining meringue mixture until blended. Spread in pan.

6. Bake in moderate oven (350°) 15 minutes, or until top springs back when lightly touched.

7. Cool in pan on wire rack for 5 minutes; loosen cake around edges of pan with a sharp knife; invert cake onto a large cooky sheet; peel off wax paper; invert onto rack; cool.

8. Make filling: Cut semisweet chocolate into small pieces. Combine with cream in a medium-size saucepan. Heat slowly, stirring constantly, until chocolate melts; remove from heat; stir in coffee liqueur. Pour into a medium-size bowl. Chill 1½ hours, or until completely cold.

9. Beat chilled chocolate-cream mixture until stiff and thick.

10. Cut cooled cake in half crosswise. Place 1 half on a small cooky sheet. Top with whipped chocolate cream, spreading to make a layer about 1½ inches thick; top with second half of cake. Chill 1 hour, or until filling is firm.

11. Make frosting: Heat sugar and coffee in a medium-size saucepan until sugar dissolves. Cut chocolate into small pieces; add to saucepan with corn syrup. Heat to boiling, stirring constantly; cook, at a slow boil, stirring constantly, 5 minutes. Remove from heat; add butter or margarine and coffee liqueur. Beat 5 minutes, or until mixture begins to thicken. Quickly spread over cake layer about ¼-inch thick. Chill at least 1 hour.

12. To serve: Cut cake into 12 squares with a heavy sharp knife; decorate each square.

Cookies: The Best of the Batch / 2

Very little needs to be said about cookies—except, perhaps, please pass the cooky jar. And it is to the stately cooky jar that we devote this chapter, one that's filled with the very best cookies imaginable. They're easy-to-make cookies, made even simpler by our supplementary how-to illustrations and two whole pages of cooky cutter patterns you'll want to use when you make rolled cookies. Try these cookies for holidays and for everyday. See if you don't agree they're the very best of the batch!

OATMEAL CRUNCHES

Bake at 375° for 12 minutes.
Makes about 4 dozen.

1½ cups sifted all-purpose flour
½ teaspoon baking soda
½ teaspoon salt
 Dash of mace
1 cup shortening
1¼ cups firmly packed brown sugar
1 egg
¼ cup milk
1¾ cups quick-cooking rolled oats
1 cup chopped walnuts
1 cup raisins

1. Measure flour, soda, salt and mace into a sifter.
2. Cream shortening with brown sugar until fluffy in a large bowl; beat in egg and milk. Sift in flour mixture, blending well to make a thick batter; fold in oats, walnuts and raisins.
3. Drop by teaspoonfuls, 3 inches apart, on greased cooky sheets.
4. Bake in moderate oven (375°) 12 minutes, or until lightly golden. Remove from cooky sheets; cool completely on wire racks.

CHINESE ALMOND COOKIES

Bake at 350° for 15 minutes.
Makes 3½ dozen cookies.

1 cup vegetable shortening
1 cup sugar
2 eggs
1 tablespoon water
3 teaspoons almond extract
3 cups sifted all-purpose flour
1½ teaspoons baking soda
¼ teaspoon salt
1 package (6 ounces) whole blanched almonds

1. Beat shortening and sugar until light and fluffy in a large bowl with electric mixer.
2. Beat eggs in a small bowl with a fork until thoroughly blended; remove 2 tablespoons egg into a cup; add 1 tablespoon water; set aside.
3. Add beaten eggs and almond extract to shortening-sugar mixture, blending thoroughly.
4. Sift flour, baking soda and salt onto wax

paper. Beat into the shortening-sugar mixture.
5. Shape into 1½-inch balls using 1 level measuring tablespoon of cooky dough. Place 2 inches apart on lightly greased cooky sheets.
6. Flatten cooky with fingertips into a 2-inch round. Place 1 blanched almond into the center of each cooky. Brush top of each cooky with reserved egg and water.
7. Bake in moderate oven (350°) 15 minutes, or until firm. Remove to wire racks to cool.

PEPPERMINT PINWHEELS

Bake at 350° for 10 minutes.
Makes 5 dozen cookies.

2 cups sifted all-purpose flour
½ teaspoon baking powder
½ teaspoon salt
¾ cup (1½ sticks) butter or margarine
¾ cup sugar
1 egg yolk
1 teaspoon vanilla
½ teaspoon mint extract
 Few drops red food coloring

1. Sift flour, baking powder and salt onto wax paper.
2. Beat butter or margarine with sugar until fluffy light in a large bowl; beat in egg yolk and vanilla.
3. Stir in flour mixture, a third at a time, blending well after each addition, to make a soft dough.
4. Divide dough in half, and to half add the peppermint extract and enough red food coloring to tint the dough a deep pink.
5. Roll out each color dough to a 16x10-inch rectangle, between sheets of wax paper. Remove top sheet of wax paper from pink dough; place dough top side down on top of plain dough; peel off paper.
6. Roll up dough tightly, jelly-roll fashion. Wrap in wax paper or foil; chill several hours until very firm. (Or you may freeze dough and take out of freezer one half hour before baking.)
7. When ready to bake, unwrap dough and cut into ¼-inch thick slices with a sharp knife; place on ungreased cooky sheets.
8. Bake in moderate oven (350°) 10 minutes, or until cookies are firm, but not browned. Remove from cooky sheets to wire racks; cool.

Left: Delicious Oatmeal Crunchies are made with oatmeal, raisins, brown sugar and nuts. The recipe is above.

DATE CHEWS

Bake at 350° for 25 minutes.
Makes about 6 dozen cookies.

    ¾ cup sifted all-purpose flour
    ½ teaspoon baking powder
    ¼ teaspoon salt
    3 eggs
    1 cup sugar (for dough)
    2 tablespoons orange juice
    1 package (8 ounces) pitted dates, chopped
    1 cup chopped pecans
    ¼ cup chopped candied orange peel
       Sugar (for coating)

1. Sift flour, baking powder and salt onto wax paper.
2. Beat eggs until foamy-light in a large bowl; slowly beat in the 1 cup sugar; continue beating until mixture is fluffy-thick. Stir in orange juice.
3. Fold in flour mixture, dates, pecans and orange peel. Spread evenly in a 13x9x2-inch buttered baking pan.
4. Bake in moderate oven (350°) 25 minutes, or until golden and top springs back when lightly pressed with fingertip. Cool in pan on a wire rack 15 minutes.
5. Cut lengthwise into 9 strips and crosswise into 8 to make 72 pieces, about 1x1½. Roll each in sugar in a pie plate to coat generously.

OUR BEST-EVER BROWNIES

Bake at 350° for 30 minutes.
Makes 16 brownies.

    2 squares unsweetened chocolate
    ½ cup (1 stick) butter or margarine
    2 eggs
    1 cup sugar
    1 teaspoon vanilla
    ½ cup sifted all-purpose flour
    ⅛ teaspoon salt
    ¾ cup chopped walnuts
    1 package (6 ounces) semisweet chocolate pieces
    ½ cup dairy sour cream

1. Melt chocolate and butter or margarine in a small saucepan over low heat; cool.
2. Beat eggs in small bowl with electric mixer until fluffy. Gradually beat in sugar until mixture is fluffy-thick. Stir in chocolate mixture and vanilla.
3. Fold in flour and salt until well-blended; stir in walnuts. Spread evenly in 8x8x2-inch buttered baking pan.
4. Bake in moderate oven (350°) 30 minutes, or until shiny and firm on top. Cool completely in pan on a wire rack.
5. Melt chocolate pieces in top of a double boiler over hot water. Stir until smooth. Remove from heat; stir in sour cream until well-blended. Spread frosting on cooled brownies. Cut into 2-inch squares.

BROWN-EDGE LEMON WAFERS

Bake at 375° for about 10 minutes.
Makes about 5 dozen 3-inch cookies.

    ¼ cup sugar
    3 teaspoons grated lemon rind
    2 cups sifted all-purpose flour
    2 teaspoons baking powder
    ½ teaspoon salt
    ½ cup shortening
    1 cup sugar
    1 egg
    ½ teaspoon vanilla
    ½ cup water
    ¼ cup lemon juice

1. Blend sugar and 1 teaspoon of the lemon rind in cup; reserve.
2. Measure flour, baking powder and salt into sifter.
3. Cream shortening in medium-size bowl until soft; gradually add sugar (for dough), creaming well after each addition.
4. Blend in egg, remaining lemon rind and vanilla; beat until mixture is light and fluffy.
5. Sift and add dry ingredients alternately with water and lemon juice, blending until smooth after each addition. Dough will be very soft.
6. Drop dough by teaspoonfuls onto buttered cooky sheets, keeping mounds about 2 inches apart. Sprinkle lightly with lemon-sugar mixture.
7. Bake in moderate oven (375°) about 10 minutes, or until edges of cookies are light brown.
8. Remove from cooky sheets; cool on wire racks. Store in tightly covered container.

GINGERBREAD COOKIES

Bake at 350° for 8 minutes.
Makes 6 dozen cookies.

5½ cups sifted all-purpose flour
  1 teaspoon baking soda
  1 teaspoon salt
  2 teaspoons ground cinnamon
  1 teaspoon ground ginger
  1 teaspoon ground cloves
  ½ teaspoon ground nutmeg
  1 cup vegetable shortening
  1 cup sugar
  1 cup molasses
  1 egg
  1 teaspoon vanilla
     Royal Frosting (recipe follows)

1. Sift flour, baking soda, salt and spices onto wax paper.
2. Beat vegetable shortening with sugar until fluffy-light in a large bowl; beat in molasses, egg and vanilla.
3. Stir in flour mixture, a third at a time, blending well after each addition, to make a soft dough. Wrap dough in foil and chill 4 hours, or overnight.
4. Roll out dough, one quarter at a time, to a ⅛-inch thickness on a lightly floured pastry board. Cut with 3-inch cooky cutters.
5. Place, approximately 1 inch apart, on ungreased cooky sheets.
6. Bake in moderate oven (350°) 8 minutes, or until cookies are firm but not too dark. Remove to wire racks with spatula; cool. Decorate with Royal Frosting and allow frosting to harden before storing.

ROYAL FROSTING

Makes about 1½ cups.

  2 egg whites
  1 teaspoon lemon juice
3½ cups sifted 10X (confectioners') sugar

Beat egg whites and lemon juice until foamy in a medium-size bowl. Slowly beat in sugar, until frosting stands in firm peaks and is stiff enough to hold a sharp line when cut through with a knife. Keep frosting covered with a damp paper towel to keep from drying before using.

FLORENTINES

Bake at 325° for 12 minutes.
Makes 2 dozen.

  ⅓ cup butter or margarine
  ⅓ cup honey
  ¼ cup sugar
  2 tablespoons milk
  ⅔ cup sifted all-purpose flour
  1 cup (8 ounces) mixed candied fruits
  1 can (3½ ounces) sliced almonds
  3 squares semisweet chocolate
  1 tablespoon butter or margarine

1. Melt ⅓ cup butter or margarine in pan; remove from heat; stir in honey, sugar, milk.
2. Add flour, candied fruits and almonds; stir until well-blended.
3. Return saucepan to very low heat. Cook, stirring constantly, until mixture begins to thicken (about 2 minutes). Remove from heat.
4. Drop mixture by teaspoonfuls, 2 inches apart, onto well-greased cooky sheets.
5. Bake in slow oven (325°) 12 minutes, or until golden-brown around edges. Cool slightly on cooky sheets, then remove and cool completely.
6. Melt chocolate squares and 1 tablespoon butter or margarine in a metal cup over simmering water. Spread the bottom of half the cookies with chocolate and top each with a second cooky. Allow to become firm before storing.

MELT-AWAYS

Bake at 325° for 20 minutes.
Makes about 4 dozen balls.

  ½ cup butter or margarine
  3 tablespoons 10X (confectioners') sugar
  1 cup sifted all-purpose flour
  1 cup finely chopped walnuts

1. Cream butter or margarine with sugar in medium-size bowl; gradually add flour, mixing in thoroughly; stir in nuts; chill.
2. Form teaspoonfuls of dough into marble-size balls by rolling lightly between palms of hands; place on ungreased cooky sheets.
3. Bake in moderate oven (325°) 20 minutes, or until pale golden.
4. Remove from cooky sheet; while still hot, roll in additional confectioners' sugar; cool.

LEMON-DATE DIAMONDS

Bake at 325° for 35 minutes.
Makes 3 dozen cookies.

1¼ cups sifted all-purpose flour
1½ teaspoons baking powder
½ teaspoon salt
½ teaspoon pumpkin-pie spice
2 eggs
1 cup granulated sugar
2 tablespoons vegetable oil
1 package (8 ounces) pitted dates, chopped
½ cup chopped pecans
1 cup 10X (confectioners') sugar
1 tablespoon milk
1 tablespoon lemon juice

1. Measure flour, baking powder, salt and pumpkin-pie spice into a sifter.
2. Beat eggs and granulated sugar just until blended in a large bowl; stir in vegetable oil, dates and pecans. Sift flour mixture over top, then blend in. Spread in a 13x9x2-inch buttered baking pan.
3. Bake in slow oven (325°) 35 minutes, or until golden and a wooden pick inserted in center comes out clean. Cool in pan on a wire rack.
4. Beat 10X sugar with milk and lemon juice until smooth in a small bowl; spread over cookies. Let stand until frosting is firm.
5. Cut into diamond shapes or bars.

ALMOND MACAROONS

Bake at 325° for 20 minutes.
Makes about 3 dozen cookies.

1 can (8 ounces) almond paste
2 egg whites
Dash of salt
1 teaspoon vanilla
1 cup sifted 10X (confectioners') sugar
Granulated sugar
Sliced almonds
Red candied cherries, quartered

1. Butter a large cooky sheet; dust with flour; tap off any excess.
2. Break up almond paste with fingers into large bowl.
3. Add egg whites, salt and vanilla. Beat with electric mixer at low speed until mixture is smooth and the ingredients are well-blended.
4. Add confectioners' sugar slowly, continuing to beat at low speed, until a soft dough forms.
5. Fit a pastry bag with a round tip. Fill bag with dough.
6. Pipe dough out in small rounds, or drop by teaspoonfuls on prepared cooky sheet. (Macaroons will spread very little when they bake.)
7. For a crackly top: Dip fingertip into water; pat over tops; sprinkle with granulated sugar. Decorate tops with almonds and cherries.
8. Bake in slow oven (325°) for 20 minutes, or until golden-brown.
9. Remove to wire racks with a spatula; cool.

WALNUT SUGARPLUMS

Makes about 2 dozen 2-ounce cakes.

1 package (8 ounces) pitted dates
1 cup seeded muscat raisins
1 jar (4 ounces) chopped candied pineapple
1 jar (4 ounces) chopped candied citron
½ cup (1 stick) butter or margarine
1 cup 10X (confectioners') sugar
2 tablespoons light corn syrup
1 tablespoon lemon juice
¼ cup finely chopped candied or crystallized ginger
2 packages (5 ounces each) shortbread cookies, crushed (about 3 cups)
2 teaspoons ground cinnamon
1 cup chopped walnuts
Walnut halves

1. Chop dates and raisins; dice pineapple and citron.
2. Cream butter or margarine with 10X sugar until fluffy-light in a large bowl; beat in corn syrup and lemon juice. Stir in dates and raisins, then pineapple, citron and ginger.
3. Mix crushed cookies, cinnamon and chopped walnuts in a medium-size bowl; sprinkle over fruit mixture; stir in until completely blended. (Mixture will be stiff.)
4. Pack into tiny souffle or nut cups (1½-ounce size). Garnish each with a walnut half. Set cups in a large shallow pan or on a tray for easy handling; cover tightly with waxed paper or transparent wrap. Chill until firm. Keep refrigerated until ready to serve or give.

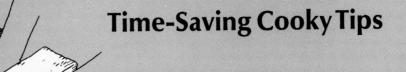

Time-Saving Cooky Tips

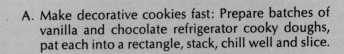

A. Make decorative cookies fast: Prepare batches of vanilla and chocolate refrigerator cooky doughs, pat each into a rectangle, stack, chill well and slice.

B. Juice cans make good molds for refrigerator cookies. Pack dough in the can and chill. At baking time, remove the bottom of the can. (Use a can opener that cuts a smooth edge.) Press against bottom to push out dough—just enough to make one $\frac{1}{8}$- to $\frac{1}{4}$-inch thick cooky. Cut with a sharp knife and place dough on an ungreased cooky sheet. Repeat procedure until all dough is used.

C. Ball cookies will be even in size if you pat the dough into a long roll first, then divide it: First in half, then quarters, then eighths and sixteenths, depending on what size cooky you want.

D. With only one batch of dough, you can make a whole plateful of different-looking treats. Here's how: After shaping the dough, leave some plain, press others, crisscross fashion with a fork. Make a hollow in some with your thumb or the handle of a wooden spoon to fill with jam after baking, or top with a big walnut half.

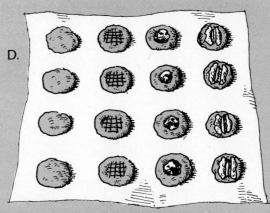

PINE NUT MACAROONS

Bake at 375° for 10 minutes.
Makes about 2½ dozen cookies.

1 cup blanched almonds
1 cup sugar
2 egg whites
½ teaspoon almond extract
1 jar (8 ounces) pine nuts (pignoli)

1. Dry blanched almonds thoroughly by placing them in a warm oven (350°) for 5 to 10 minutes. Grind as fine as possible, until powdery, while still warm.
2. Combine ground almonds and sugar in a medium-size bowl; add unbeaten egg whites and almond extract; beat thoroughly.
3. Drop by teaspoonfuls onto generously buttered and floured cooky sheets, leaving 1 inch between cookies. Smooth into rounds. Top each cooky with approximately ½ teaspoon pine nuts, pressing nuts into cooky. Let stand 3 hours.
4. Bake in moderate oven (375°) for 10 minutes. Remove cookies from oven; let stand on cooky sheets for 5 minutes; carefully remove with wide spatula (if cookies stiffen, put back into oven for a few seconds to soften). Store in airtight container when thoroughly cooled.

SPRINGERLE

Bake at 300° for 15 minutes.
Makes about 6 dozen small square cookies or about 3 dozen larger rectangles.

Anise seeds
4 eggs
2 cups sugar
4 cups sifted all-purpose flour
1 teaspoon baking soda
2 teaspoons anise extract

1. Butter cooky sheets; sprinkle with anise seeds.
2. Beat eggs with sugar until fluffy-light and thick in a large bowl. (Beating will take 5 minutes with an electric mixer. This step is important so your cookies will have a frosty top layer.) Stir in flour, a third at a time, soda and anise extract, blending well to form a stiff dough.
3. Roll out, about a third at a time, ½-inch thick, on a lightly floured pastry cloth or board with a plain rolling pin.
4. Flour springerle rolling pin or individual molds. Roll pin slowly only once over dough; pressing down firmly enough to make clear designs. Dough will now be about ¼-inch thick. If using individual molds, press firmly into dough; carefully lift off mold.
5. Cut along lines to separate designs. Cut around borders of individual designs. Lift each cooky carefully; moisten bottom with a drop of water. Place 1 inch apart on prepared cooky sheets. Brush excess flour from tops.
6. Let cookies stand, uncovered, overnight.
7. Bake in slow oven (300°) 15 minutes, or until firm and dry. (Cookies should not brown.) Remove to wire racks; cool. Store in a tightly covered container about a week to mellow.

CRISP MOLASSES COOKIES

Bake at 350° for 8 minutes.
Makes 8 dozen cookies.

3¾ cups sifted all-purpose flour
1 teaspoon baking soda
½ teaspoon salt
2 tablespoons cocoa
2 teaspoons ground ginger
1 tablespoon ground cinnamon
2 teaspoons ground cloves
1 cup (2 sticks) butter or margarine, softened
1 cup sugar
1 egg
½ cup molasses
Royal Frosting (recipe on page 37)

1. Sift flour, baking soda, salt, cocoa, ginger, cinnamon and cloves onto wax paper.
2. Beat butter or margarine until fluffy; add sugar gradually, beating well after each addition. Add egg and molasses; beat well. Stir in flour mixture; blend well. Wrap in plastic wrap or foil; refrigerate several hours, or overnight.
3. Roll out small portions of dough on a floured pastry board; cut into plain or fancy shapes with cooky cutters; brush excess flour off dough. Place on lightly buttered cooky sheets.
4. Bake in moderate oven (350°) for 8 minutes, or until edges are browned. Let cookies cool a few minutes on cooky sheets. Remove to wire racks with spatula; cool.

From left to right on opposite page:
German Gingerbread Cookies, Florentines, Springerles,
Pine Nut Macaroons, Lebkuchen and Peppermint Pinwheels.
Recipes are in this chapter.

Cooky Cutter
Patterns You Can Trace

Using tissue or tracing paper, trace the designs shown here; cut out and glue onto cardboard. Cut the cardboard with scissors or a razor blade, and you have your own cooky cutters! When you use these cardboard cutters, place them on top of rolled dough, hold in place and cut around cardboard with a sharp knife. Transfer cutout dough to cooky sheet and bake according to recipe directions.

SUGAR COOKIES

Bake at 375° for 10 minutes.
Makes 4½ dozen cookies.

1 cup (2 sticks) butter or margarine, softened
1 cup sugar
2 eggs, room temperature
2½ teaspoons vanilla
3½ cups sifted all-purpose flour
2¼ teaspoons baking powder
¼ teaspoon salt

1. Beat butter or margarine and sugar in a large bowl at high speed on electric mixer. Add eggs and vanilla; beat until light and fluffy.
2. Sift flour, baking powder and salt onto wax paper. Stir into butter-sugar mixture.
3. Shape dough into 1-inch balls (1 level tablespoon). Place on lightly buttered cooky sheets.
4. Butter bottom of glass or jar, dip in the 3 tablespoons sugar. Flatten each cooky to ¼ inch thickness with bottom of glass.
5. Bake in moderate oven (375°) 10 minutes, or until edges are lightly browned. Cool.

LEBKUCHEN

Bake at 350° for 10 minutes.
Makes about 5 dozen cookies.

¾ cup honey
¾ cup firmly packed dark brown sugar
1 egg
2 teaspoons grated lemon rind
3 tablespoons lemon juice
3½ cups sifted all-purpose flour
1 teaspoon salt
1 teaspoon ground cinnamon
1 teaspoon ground nutmeg
½ teaspoon ground allspice
½ teaspoon ground ginger
¼ teaspoon ground cloves
½ teaspoon baking soda
1 cup (8 ounces) citron, finely chopped
1 cup chopped unblanched almonds
Sugar Glaze (recipe follows)

1. Heat honey to boiling in a small saucepan; pour into a large bowl. Cool about 30 minutes.
2. Stir brown sugar, egg, lemon rind and lemon juice into cooled honey; blend well.
3. Sift flour, salt, cinnamon, nutmeg, allspice, ginger, cloves and baking soda onto wax paper. Stir into honey mixture a third at a time. Add citron and almonds. Dough will be stiff but sticky. Wrap in foil or transparent wrap; refrigerate several hours, or until firm.
4. Roll out dough, ⅛ at a time, on a lightly floured pastry board, to a 6x5-inch rectangle. Cut into 8 rectangles, 2½x1½ inches. Place 1 inch apart on greased cooky sheets.
5. Bake in moderate oven (350°) 10 minutes, or until firm. Remove to wire racks.
6. While cookies are hot, brush with hot Sugar Glaze. When cookies are cool, decorate with almond halves, candied cherry halves and pieces of citron, if you wish. Use confectioners' sugar and water mixed to a smooth paste as "glue." Store cookies in wax-paper-separated layers in a covered container for 2 weeks to mellow.

SUGAR GLAZE: Combine ¾ cup granulated sugar and ⅓ cup water in a saucepan. Bring to boiling; lower heat; simmer 3 minutes. Remove from heat; stir in ¼ cup 10X (confectioners') sugar. Makes about ¾ cup.

CHOCOLATE CHIP COOKIES

Bake at 375° for 10 minutes.
Makes 4½ dozen cookies.

¾ cup (1½ sticks) butter or margarine
½ cup sugar
½ cup firmly packed brown sugar
1 egg
1 teaspoon vanilla
2 cups sifted all-purpose flour
½ teaspoon baking soda
¼ teaspoon salt
1 package (6 ounces) semisweet chocolate pieces
½ cup coarsely chopped walnuts

1. Beat butter or margarine, sugars, egg and vanilla in a large bowl with an electric mixer until light and fluffy.
2. Sift flour, baking soda and salt onto wax paper. Beat into butter-sugar mixture. Stir in chocolate pieces and walnuts.
3. Drop by teaspoonfuls onto buttered cooky sheets. Bake in moderate oven (375°) 10 minutes, or until cookies are lightly browned. Remove with spatula to wire racks to cool.

Dunked in sugar, drizzled with glaze, sprinkled
with coconut or dipped in chocolate,
there's absolutely nothing more irresistible than
a doughnut—with or without the hole!
The following collection of recipes not only bears
this statement out, but proves doughnuts
are also easy, fun and frivolous to make. See if
you don't agree when you make the
ever-popular jelly doughnut, the aristocratic
French cruller and the basic old-fashioned
doughnut. (It's the kind you can twirl on your finger,
dunk in your coffee and reminisce about long
after the doughnut plate is wiped clean.)

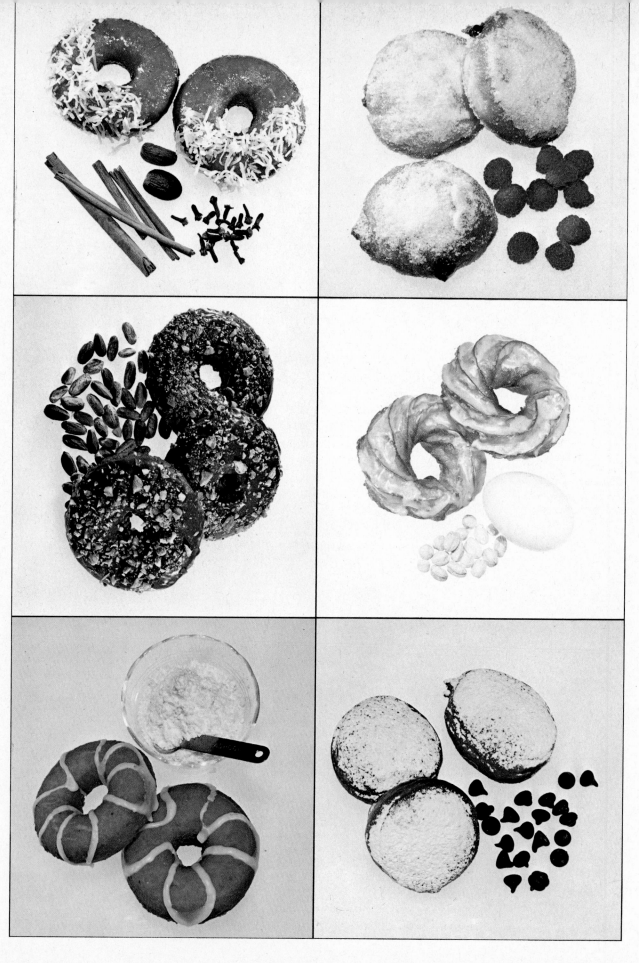

From left to right, top to bottom: Coconut Honey-Spiced Doughnuts, Jelly Doughnuts, Chocolate-Nut Doughnuts, French Crullers, Old-Fashioned Doughnuts and Doubloons. Recipes are in this chapter.

JELLY DOUGHNUTS

Makes 16 doughnuts.

    1 package (13¾ ounces) hot-roll mix
    ¾ cup sugar
    ¾ cup very warm water
    1 jar (12 ounces) strawberry preserves
      Vegetable oil (for frying)

1. Prepare hot-roll mix with 3 tablespoons of the sugar and water and let rise, following label directions.
2. Turn dough out onto a lightly floured pastry board; knead 8 to 10 times. Roll out ½ inch thick; cut with a floured 2½-inch cooky cutter; place on a lightly floured pastry board or cooky sheet. Reroll and cut out all leftover dough.
3. Cover with a clean towel; let rise 30 minutes, or until double in bulk.
4. Fill a large heavy saucepan or electric skillet ⅔ full with vegetable oil. Heat to 370° on a deep-fat thermometer. Drop doughnuts, 2 to 3 at a time, into oil. Fry, turning once, 3 minutes, or until golden. Drop hot doughnuts into bowl with remaining sugar; coat well. Drain on paper toweling; cool.
5. Cut a slit in one side of each doughnut. Fill pastry bag with preserves; place tip into slit and fill each doughnut.

FRENCH CRULLERS

Makes about 12 crullers.

    ¼ cup granulated sugar
    ½ teaspoon salt
    ¼ cup shortening
    1 cup hot water
    1 cup sifted all-purpose flour
    3 eggs
      Vegetable oil (for frying)
    ¾ cup sifted 10X (confectioners') sugar
    ½ teaspoon vanilla
    ⅛ teaspoon ground cardamom
    3 to 4 teaspoons water

1. Measure sugar, salt and shortening into a saucepan. Add hot water; bring to boiling.
2. Add flour all at once; stir vigorously until mixture leaves side of pan. Remove from heat. Add eggs, one at a time, beating well after each.
3. Cut 12 three-inch squares of foil; grease each. Fit pastry bag with a large rosette tube; fill with dough. Press a 2½-inch ring of dough onto each foil square. Let stand 15 minutes.
4. Fill a large heavy saucepan or electric skillet ⅔ full with vegetable oil. Heat to 370° on a deep-fat thermometer. Hold ring of dough close to surface of oil; carefully slip from foil into oil. Fry 3 at a time, turning once, about 3 to 5 minutes, or until crullers are golden and puffed. Drain on paper toweling.
5. When crullers are cool, mix 10X sugar, vanilla, cardamom and water. Drizzle over crullers.

COCONUT HONEY-SPICED DOUGHNUTS

Makes about 16 doughnuts.

    3¾ cups sifted all-purpose flour
    2 teaspoons baking powder
    1 teaspoon baking soda
    1 teaspoon ground cinnamon
    ½ teaspoon ground nutmeg
    ¼ teaspoon ground cloves
    ¼ teaspoon salt
    1 cup sugar
    2 eggs
    3 tablespoons shortening
    ¾ cup buttermilk
      Vegetable oil (for frying)
    1 cup honey
    ½ cup flaked coconut

1. Sift flour, baking powder, baking soda, cinnamon, nutmeg, cloves and salt onto wax paper.
2. Beat sugar, eggs and shortening at medium speed with mixer until fluffy; blend in milk.
3. Remove bowl from mixer; stir in dry ingredients until well-blended.
4. Wrap dough in wax paper; chill 2 hours.
5. Place dough on a lightly floured pastry board and roll to a ½ inch thickness. Cut out with a lightly floured doughnut cutter.
6. Fill a large heavy saucepan or electric skillet ⅔ full with vegetable oil. Heat to 370° on a deep-fat thermometer.
7. Drop doughnuts, 2 or 3 at a time, into oil. Fry, turning once, 3 minutes, or until golden. Drain on paper toweling.
8. Heat honey slowly to boiling in a medium-size saucepan. Dip doughnuts into honey; coat well. Sprinkle coconut onto wax paper; dip half of each doughnut into coconut.

OLD-FASHIONED DOUGHNUTS

Makes about 16 doughnuts.

3¾ cups sifted all-purpose flour
4 teaspoons baking powder
½ teaspoon ground mace
¼ teaspoon salt
1 cup granulated sugar
2 eggs
3 tablespoons shortening
¾ cup milk
1 teaspoon vanilla
Vegetable oil (for frying)
¾ cup sifted 10X (confectioners') sugar
2 teaspoons warm water

1. Sift flour, powder, mace, salt onto wax paper.
2. Beat sugar, eggs and shortening at medium speed in large bowl with electric mixer until fluffy; blend in milk and vanilla.
3. Remove bowl from mixer and stir in flour mixture until well-blended.
4. Wrap dough in wax paper; chill for 2 hours.
5. Place dough on a lightly floured pastry board and roll to a ½-inch thickness. Cut out with a lightly floured doughnut cutter.
6. Fill a large heavy saucepan or electric skillet ⅔ full with vegetable oil. Heat to 370° on a deep-fat thermometer.
7. Drop doughnuts, 2 or 3 at a time, into hot oil. Fry, turning once, 3 minutes, or until golden. Drain on paper toweling; cool.
8. Combine 10X sugar and water in a cup. Drizzle over cooled doughnuts.

CHOCOLATE DOUBLOONS

Makes 18 doughnuts.

1 package (13¾ ounces) hot-roll mix
¾ cup very warm water
3 tablespoons granulated sugar
1 egg
⅔ cup semisweet chocolate pieces
1 egg white, slightly beaten
Vegetable oil (for frying)
10X (confectioners') sugar

1. Prepare hot-roll mix with water, sugar and egg and let rise, following label directions.
2. Turn dough out onto a lightly floured board; knead 8 to 10 times. Roll out ¼ inch thick; cut

into 36 rounds with a two-inch cooky cutter.
3. Divide the semisweet chocolate pieces evenly over half of the rounds, clustering pieces in the centers. Brush edges of rounds with beaten egg white; top each with a plain round. Press edges together. Place on floured cooky sheet.
4. Cover with a towel; let rise 30 minutes, or until double in bulk.
5. Fill a large heavy saucepan or electric skillet ⅔ full with vegetable oil. Heat to 370° on a deep-fat thermometer. Drop doughnuts, 3 at a time, raised side down, into oil. Fry, turning once, about 3 minutes, or until golden; drain.
6. When cool, roll doughnuts in 10X sugar.

CHOCOLATE-NUT DOUGHNUTS

Makes 16 doughnuts.

2 squares unsweetened chocolate
2 tablespoons shortening
3¾ cups sifted all-purpose flour
4 teaspoons baking powder
½ teaspoon salt
2 eggs
1 cup sugar
¾ cup milk
1 teaspoon vanilla
Vegetable oil (for frying)
1 package (6 ounces) chocolate glaze mix
½ cup chopped pistachio nuts

1. Combine chocolate and shortening in top of a double boiler; place over simmering water; stir until melted; cool. Reserve.
2. Sift flour, powder and salt onto wax paper.
3. Beat eggs and sugar in large bowl with electric mixer at medium until fluffy. Beat in vanilla and chocolate. Remove bowl from mixer.
4. Stir in flour mixture until well-blended. Wrap in plastic wrap or wax paper; chill 2 hours.
5. Roll out dough to ½-inch thickness on a lightly floured pastry board. Cut with floured doughnut cutter; reroll and cut leftover dough.
6. Fill a large heavy saucepan or electric skillet ⅔ full with vegetable oil. Heat to 370° on a deep-fat thermometer. Drop doughnuts, about 3 at a time, into oil; fry, turning once, 3 to 5 minutes, or until firm. Drain on toweling; cool.
7. Prepare chocolate glaze mix, following label directions. Dip each doughnut into glaze; sprinkle with nuts. Place on a rack; let glaze set.

Puddings & Custards /4

From old-fashioned Steamed Date-Walnut Pudding to super speedy Italian Zabaglione, there's nothing quite like homemade pudding or custard. It offers unique flavor possibilities and while it's not always quick to make, it's not difficult either. Most of the time, as you'll see from the following pages of recipes, the most difficult thing about pudding is in hungrily waiting for it to bake, steam or take shape in the refrigerator. (On page 52 we've included some special tips on gelatin molds.) Once the waiting's over, the joy begins!

CHOCOLATE BLANC-MANGE

Makes 6 servings.

  1 cup sugar
  ⅓ cup cornstarch
  ¼ teaspoon salt
  3 squares unsweetened chocolate, cut up
  3 cups milk
  1½ teaspoons vanilla

1. Combine sugar, cornstarch, salt and chocolate in medium-size pan; gradually stir in milk.
2. Cook over medium heat, stirring constantly, until chocolate melts and mixture comes to boiling and is thickened. Boil 1 minute. Remove from heat; stir in vanilla. Pour into a 3-cup mold. Cover with plastic wrap; refrigerate until cold, about 3 hours.
3. When ready to serve, run a knife around top; dip mold very quickly in and out of hot water. Cover with serving plate; turn upside down; shake gently; lift off mold. Garnish with whipped cream and maraschino cherries, if desired.

STEAMED DATE-WALNUT PUDDING

Steam for 2 hours and 30 minutes.
Makes 8 servings.

  1½ cups sifted all-purpose flour
  1 teaspoon baking powder
  ¾ teaspoon baking soda
  ½ teaspoon salt
  ¼ teaspoon ground cinnamon
  ⅛ teaspoon mace
  1 egg
  ½ cup sugar
  3 tablespoons butter or margarine
  1 cup orange juice
  ¼ cup orange marmalade
  1 tablespoon grated lemon rind
  1 teaspoon vanilla
  1 cup chopped walnuts
  1 cup chopped dates
  ½ cup candied cherries, chopped
  Hard-Sauce Pinwheels (recipe follows)

1. Butter a 6-cup pudding mold or heat-proof bowl; sprinkle with sugar.
2. Sift flour, baking powder, baking soda, salt, cinnamon and mace on wax paper.
3. Beat egg in a large bowl; beat in sugar, butter or margarine, orange juice, marmalade, lemon rind and vanilla.
4. Combine walnuts, dates and cherries with flour mixture; stir into egg mixture. Turn into prepared mold or bowl; cover with lid of mold or with foil, or a double thickness of wax paper and fasten with string to hold tightly.
5. Place on rack in a large kettle (or, make a doughnut shape of crumpled foil to fit bottom of kettle to serve as a rack); pour in boiling water to half-way point on mold. Cover kettle. Keep water gently boiling; add more boiling water, if necessary. Steam 2½ hours.
6. Cool pudding 10 minutes on wire rack; turn out onto serving plate. Serve warm with Hard-Sauce Pinwheels.
7. To reheat: Place pudding on sheet of heavy foil; bring foil up and gather at top, folding securely, to make pouch. Place pudding on rack in same kettle it was cooked in. Pour 2 inches of boiling water into kettle; cover; simmer for 30 minutes, or until heated through.

HARD-SAUCE PINWHEELS

Makes 8 servings.

  ½ cup (1 stick) butter or margarine, softened
  2 cups sifted 10X (confectioners') sugar
  2 tablespoons brandy
  Red food coloring

1. Beat butter or margarine until fluffy in small bowl of electric mixer. Gradually beat in confectioners' sugar and brandy.
2. Divide mixture in half; tint 1 portion deep pink (the color will deepen somewhat as mixture stands).
3. Turn both tinted and plain portions onto separate sheets of wax paper; spread into rectangles. Cover with second sheets of wax paper; refrigerate. Carefully roll both portions of hard sauce between wax paper sheets to equal size rectangles, about ⅜-inch thick; refrigerate the rectangles again.
4. Remove top wax paper sheets; invert pink portion on plain portion. Remove wax paper. Carefully roll up from long side with help of bottom sheet of wax paper; wrap tightly in fresh wax paper sheet (roll, rather than try to lift finished roll, onto the fresh sheet). Refrigerate several hours, or overnight. Cut into slices and arrange around the Date-Walnut Pudding.

Left: Chocolate Blanc-Mange, an old-fashioned favorite that's easy on the chef. The recipe is included in this chapter.

Gelatin Mold Tricks You Should Know

1. Chill gelatin base fast by placing bowl in a pan of ice and water. Gelatin sets first at the bottom and side, so stir it often for even thickening.

2. Puzzled about the size of a fancy mold? Figure it out by filling the mold right to the brim with measured amounts of water. The total gives you the cup-size of mold.

3. To unmold gelatin, follow these steps: (A) Break the vacuum at the bottom of mold so that the dessert will slip out easily. First run a small-tip knife around top edge of mold to loosen. (B) Then tip mold from side to side, shaking gently, until gelatin pulls away completely. (C) Cover mold with serving plate; grasp both firmly; turn upside down; lift off mold. An alternate method (not shown): Loosen with knife as above, dip mold quickly in and out of hot water, and invert onto plate.

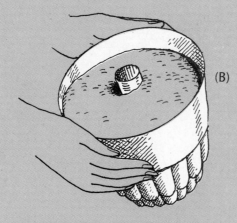

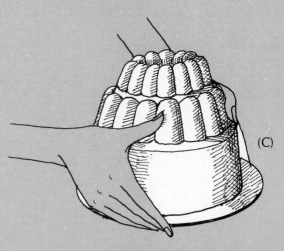

HOLIDAY PLUM PUDDING

Steam for 5 hours and 30 minutes.
Makes 12 to 16 servings.

 1 package (8 ounces) pitted dates
 1 package (8 ounces) dried figs
 1 package (8 ounces) dried apricots
 ½ pound walnuts
 1 package (15 ounces) raisins
 1 jar (4 ounces) chopped candied citron
 1 cup sifted all-purpose flour
 3 teaspoons pumpkin-pie spice
 1 teaspoon salt
 4 eggs
 1 cup firmly-packed light brown sugar
 ½ pound ground suet
2½ cups soft white bread crumbs (5 slices)
 ½ cup brandy
 ½ cup corn syrup
 Eggnog Sauce (recipe follows)

1. Butter a 10-cup mold; dust evenly with granulated sugar, tapping out any excess.
2. Chop dates, figs, apricots and walnuts into small pieces. Combine with raisins and candied citron in a very large bowl.
3. Sift flour, pumpkin-pie spice and salt onto wax paper.
4. Beat eggs and brown sugar in large bowl of electric mixer at high speed, 3 minutes, until fluffy; lower speed and mix in ground suet, bread crumbs, brandy and corn syrup. Stir in flour mixture until well blended.
5. Pour egg mixture over fruits and nuts and stir until well blended. Spoon into prepared mold. Cover with lid of mold or with foil, or a double thickness of wax paper and fasten with string to hold tightly.
6. Place mold on a rack or trivet in a kettle or steamer (or, make a doughnut shape of crumpled foil to fill bottom of kettle to serve as a rack); pour in boiling water to half the depth of pudding mold; cover tightly.
7. Steam 5½ hours, or until pudding is firm and a long skewer inserted in center comes out clean. (Keep water boiling gently during entire cooking time, adding more boiling water, if needed.)
8. Cool pudding in mold 30 minutes. Loosen around edge with a knife; invert onto wire rack. Serve with Eggnog Sauce.
9. To reheat: Follow directions for Steamed Date-Walnut Pudding (recipe is on page 51).

EGGNOG SAUCE

Makes about 2 cups.

 2 egg yolks
 ½ cup sugar
 1 tablespoon flour
 Dash of salt
 2 tablespoons heavy cream
 ¼ cup (½ stick) butter or margarine, softened
 2 tablespoons brandy
 ½ cup heavy cream

1. Beat egg yolks and sugar until thick and lemon-colored in top of double boiler; stir in flour, salt and the 2 tablespoons cream.
2. Cook over simmering water, adding butter or margarine, 1 tablespoon at a time, stirring constantly, 10 minutes, or until butter melts and sauce thickens. Remove from heat; add brandy; cover; chill.
3. To serve: Beat remaining cream until stiff in a small bowl; fold into chilled egg mixture. Serve sauce with Holiday Plum Pudding.

YANKEE FRUIT COBBLER

Bake at 400° for 50 minutes.
Makes 8 servings.

 6 medium-size apples
1½ cups sugar
 ⅓ cup flour
 ½ teaspoon ground nutmeg
 2 cups cranberry-juice cocktail
 2 cups biscuit mix
 ⅔ cup milk
 1 teaspoon grated lemon rind

1. Pare apples, quarter, core and slice into a shallow 8-cup baking dish. Combine 1¼ cups of the sugar, flour and nutmeg in a small bowl; stir in cranberry juice until smooth. Pour over apples; cover.
2. Bake in hot oven (400°) 30 minutes, or until apples are tender.
3. Combine biscuit mix, 2 tablespoons of the remaining sugar, and milk in a medium-size bowl; stir just until evenly moist. Drop by tablespoonfuls in 8 mounds over hot apples. Mix remaining 2 tablespoons sugar and lemon rind in a cup; sprinkle over biscuits.
4. Bake 20 minutes longer, or until biscuits are golden. Serve the cobbler while still warm.

CREME BRULEE

Bake at 300° for 1 hour and 15 minutes.
Makes 4 servings.

  2 cups light cream or table cream
¼ cup granulated sugar
¼ teaspoon salt
  2 eggs
1½ teaspoons vanilla
  2 tablespoons brown sugar

1. Heat cream to scalding in top of a double boiler over simmering water; stir in granulated sugar and salt; remove from heat.
2. Beat eggs slightly in a medium-size bowl; slowly stir in scalded cream mixture and vanilla. Strain into a broilerproof shallow 3-cup baking dish.
3. Set dish in a large pan; place on oven shelf; pour boiling water into pan to within 1 inch of top of dish.
4. Bake in slow oven (300°) 1 hour and 15 minutes, or until center is almost set but still soft. (Do not overbake; custard will set as it cools.) Remove from water; cool; chill.
5. Just before serving, press brown sugar through a sieve on top of chilled custard. Place dish in a pan of ice. Broil 3 to 4 minutes, or until sugar starts to melt and bubble up. Spoon into dessert dishes.

ORANGE UPSIDE-DOWN PUDDING

Bake at 325° for 30 minutes.
Makes 6 servings.

  2 eggs, separated
½ cup sugar
  4 tablespoons (½ stick) butter or margarine
¼ cup thawed undiluted frozen orange juice concentrate
½ teaspoon vanilla
  2 tablespoons flour
¼ teaspoon salt
  1 cup milk

1. Beat egg whites until foamy-white and double in volume in a small bowl; beat in 2 tablespoons of the sugar, 1 tablespoon at a time, until meringue stands in firm peaks.
2. Cream butter or margarine with remaining sugar until fluffy in a medium-size bowl; beat

in egg yolks, thawed orange juice and vanilla.
3. Stir in flour and salt, then slowly stir in milk. Gently stir in meringue until fluffy-smooth; spoon into 6 buttered 6-ounce custard cups.
4. Set cups in a large shallow pan; place on oven shelf; pour boiling water into pan to depth of an inch.
5. Bake in slow oven (325°) 30 minutes, or until tops spring back when lightly pressed with fingertip. Remove cups from pan of water; cool.
6. To unmold, loosen puddings around edge with a knife; invert into serving dishes. Serve warm or cold.

CUSTARD CROWN

Bake at 325° for 2 hours.
Makes 8 servings.

¼ cup golden raisins
  1 jar (4 ounces) chopped candied pineapple
¼ cup apricot preserves
  2 packages (3 ounces each) ladyfingers
  6 eggs
½ cup sugar (for custard)
2½ cups milk
¼ cup Cointreau
  1 cup heavy cream
  2 tablespoons sugar (for cream)
  1 teaspoon vanilla

1. Place raisins in a small saucepan; cover with water. Heat to boiling; remove from heat. Let stand 5 minutes; drain.
2. Chop raisins with pineapple and preserves until almost smooth and pastelike.
3. Butter a straight-side 6-cup mold; line bottom with waxed paper. Separate ladyfingers; lay enough in mold to cover bottom; spread with 3 tablespoons of the fruit mixture. (A spoon makes the job go fast.) Stand more ladyfingers, touching each other, around side of mold to line completely.
4. Beat eggs slightly in a medium-size bowl; stir in the ½ cup sugar, milk and Cointreau.
5. Ladle 1 cup of the custard mixture into mold. Top with another layer of ladyfingers, spread with 3 tablespoons fruit mixture, and pour in ½ cup custard mixture. Continue layering with remaining ladyfingers and fruit and custard mixtures until all are used.
6. Cover mold with foil, transparent wrap or double-thick waxed paper; tie with string.

7. Set mold in a large pan; place on oven shelf; pour boiling water into pan to within 1 inch of top of mold.
8. Bake in slow oven (325°) 2 hours, or until firm on top.
9. Cool on wire rack 1 hour, then chill at least 4 hours, or even overnight.
10. To unmold, loosen dessert around edge with a small knife; invert onto a serving plate; lift off mold.
11. Beat cream with the 2 tablespoons sugar and vanilla until stiff in a medium-size bowl. Fit a fancy tip onto a pastry bag; spoon whipped cream into bag. Press out in ribbons around side of mold and in circles of rosettes on top, building up to a peak.
12. Garnish mold with a tiny wedge of green candied pineapple, if you wish.

MOCHA UPSIDE-DOWN PUDDING

Bake at 350° for 35 minutes.
Makes 6 to 8 servings.

4 tablespoons (½ stick) butter or margarine
1 cup sifted all-purpose flour
¾ cup sugar
3 tablespoons instant coffee
1½ teaspoons baking powder
Dash of salt
1 egg
½ cup milk
½ cup instant cocoa mix
1¼ cups boiling water

1. Melt butter or margarine in a small saucepan; cool.
2. Mix flour, ½ cup of the sugar, instant coffee, baking powder and salt in a large bowl.
3. Beat egg slightly in a small bowl; stir in milk and cooled butter or margarine; blend into flour mixture until smooth. Pour into a buttered 6-cup baking dish.
4. Combine cocoa mix and remaining ¼ cup sugar in a small bowl; sprinkle over batter; pour boiling water slowly over top.
5. Bake in moderate oven (350°) 35 minutes, or until center springs back when lightly pressed with fingertip. Cool 15 minutes; spoon into serving dishes, topping each with some of the sauce. Serve the pudding while still warm with cream or vanilla ice cream, if you wish.

RAISIN-BREAD PUDDING

Bake at 350° for 45 minutes.
Makes 4 servings.

2 cups milk, scalded
2 tablespoons butter or margarine
¼ cup sugar
2 eggs
2 teaspoons vanilla
6 slices raisin bread, cubed

1. Combine milk, butter or margarine, and sugar in a small bowl.
2. Beat eggs slightly in a medium-size bowl; slowly stir in milk mixture and vanilla. Pour over bread in a buttered 4-cup baking dish. Let stand 15 minutes.
3. Set baking dish in a shallow pan; place on oven shelf; pour boiling water into pan to a depth of 1 inch.
4. Bake in moderate oven (350°) 45 minutes, or until puffy-firm. Serve warm with cream.

SPICED BREAD PUDDING

Bake at 350° for 45 minutes.
Makes 6 servings.

3 cups milk, scalded
3 tablespoons butter or margarine
3 cups fresh white-bread crumbs
⅓ cup presweetened wheat germ
½ teaspoon ground cinnamon
¼ teaspoon ground nutmeg
¼ teaspoon salt
3 eggs
⅓ cup firmly packed light brown sugar
1 teaspoon vanilla

1. Combine milk and butter or margarine in a large bowl. Stir in crumbs, wheat germ, spices and salt; let stand 5 minutes; beat til smooth.
2. Beat eggs slightly in a large bowl; stir in brown sugar, vanilla and bread mixture. Let stand 15 minutes. Spoon into 6 six-ounce buttered baking dishes.
3. Set baking dishes in a shallow pan; place on oven shelf; pour boiling water into pan to a depth of 1 inch.
4. Bake in moderate oven (350°) 45 minutes, or until set. Serve warm with whipped cream sprinkled with some presweetened wheat germ.

ZABAGLIONE

Makes about 3 cups.

⅔ **cup dry white wine**
⅓ **cup sugar**
4 **egg yolks**

1. Pour wine over sugar in a large metal bowl set over a saucepan of simmering water. Bottom should not touch the water. (Or use a metal double boiler with a wide top.) Add egg yolks.
2. Cook over simmering water, beating constantly with an electric beater at low speed, 5 minutes, or just until mixture mounds slightly; remove bowl from pan of water at once.
3. Continue beating at low speed 5 minutes longer, or until mixture is almost cold. Serve in stemmed glasses, or cover and chill to serve over fruit. Chill no longer than 3 hours so sauce holds its airy-lightness.

HOLIDAY STEAMED FIG PUDDING

Makes 8 servings.

1 **package (8 ounces) dried figs**
½ **cup (1 stick) butter or margarine**
¾ **cup sugar**
3 **eggs**
½ **cup cream sherry**
¼ **cup molasses**
1 **teaspoon ground cinnamon**
½ **teaspoon salt**
4 **slices slightly dried bread, crumbled**
1 **cup chopped pecans**
Foamy Sauce (recipe follows)

1. Rinse figs; drain. Place in a small saucepan and cover with water. Heat to boiling; reduce heat and simmer 35 minutes. Remove from liquid and cool until easy to handle; chop into tiny pieces.
2. Beat butter or margarine, sugar and eggs together in a large bowl of mixer, at high speed for 3 minutes, until light and fluffy.
3. Stir in sherry, molasses, cinnamon and salt (mixture will look curdled). Add bread crumbs, figs and pecans; stir until well-blended.
4. Grease a 4-cup mold; sprinkle with sugar. Spoon mixture into mold. Cover the top of mold with a double thickness of foil; tie foil around mold with a string to seal tightly.

5. Place mold on a rack or trivet (or make a "ring" of crumpled foil) in a kettle or steamer; pour in boiling water to half the depth of pudding mold; cover kettle tightly.
6. Steam 3 hours, or until a long thin metal skewer inserted near center comes out clean. (Keep water boiling gently during entire cooking time, adding more boiling water, if needed.)
7. Cool mold 5 minutes; loosen pudding around edge with a knife; unmold onto serving plate; cool slightly. Spoon Foamy Sauce over and serve.
NOTE: Pudding can be made ahead of time and stored, when cool, wrapped in foil. To reheat pudding, keep wrapped in foil; place on cooky sheet; heat in moderate oven (350°) for 20 minutes.

FOAMY SAUCE

Makes about 3 cups.

1 **egg**
⅓ **cup butter or margarine, melted**
1½ **cups 10X (confectioners') sugar**
1 **teaspoon vanilla**
1 **teaspoon rum extract**
1 **cup heavy cream**

1. Beat egg until thick in a medium-size bowl; gradually beat in melted butter or margarine until well-blended. Stir in 10X sugar with vanilla and rum extract until smooth.
2. Beat cream until stiff in a second bowl. Fold cream into sugar mixture. Chill until serving time. Spoon some sauce over pudding and pass the remaining sauce in a bowl.

PEACH IMPERATRICE

Makes 6 servings.

1 **cup cooked regular rice**
1½ **cups milk**
1 **can (1 pound, 13 ounces) sliced cling peaches, drained**
½ **cup sugar**
1 **envelope unflavored gelatin**
3 **egg yolks**
1 **cup heavy cream**

1. Combine rice and 1 cup of the milk in a small saucepan. Heat slowly, stirring constantly,

56

until all milk is absorbed; spoon into a bowl.
2. Set aside 8 to 10 peach slices; mash remainder in a small bowl.
3. Mix sugar and gelatin in a medium-size saucepan; beat in egg yolks, peach puree and remaining ½ cup milk. Heat slowly, stirring constantly, to boiling; fold into rice mixture. Chill, stirring often, until completely cold.
4. Beat cream until stiff in a medium-size bowl. Fold into chilled peach mixture; spoon into a 6-cup mold. Chill several hours, or until firm.
5. Unmold onto a serving plate. Garnish with additional whipped cream and saved peaches.

QUEEN OF PUDDINGS

Bake at 350° for 1 hour.
Makes 6 servings.

  4 eggs
  ¾ cup sugar
    Dash of salt
  ¼ teaspoon ground cinnamon
  2 teaspoons vanilla
  1 tablespoon butter or margarine, melted
  4 cups milk
  4 cups cubed white bread (10 slices)
  1 cup apricot preserves
  ½ cup strawberry preserves

1. Separate 2 eggs; reserve egg whites. Combine egg yolks, remaining 2 eggs, ½ cup of sugar, salt, cinnamon, vanilla and butter or margarine in a large bowl; stir in milk. Place bread cubes in a lightly buttered 8-cup baking dish; pour egg mixture over the bread cubes and let stand for 15 minutes.
2. Set dish in a baking pan; place on oven rack; pour boiling water into pan to depth of one inch.
3. Bake in moderate oven (350°) 50 minutes, or until knife inserted ½ inch from edge of pudding comes out clean. (Center will be almost set, but still soft. Do not overbake, for custard will set as it cools.)
4. Beat egg whites until foamy-white and double in volume in a small bowl; beat in remaining ¼ cup sugar, 1 tablespoon at a time, until meringue stands in firm peaks.
5. Spoon ½ cup apricot preserves over hot pudding. Using a pastry bag with a large notched tip, press meringue into puffs on top of pudding, as close together as possible, so no pudding shows. (This will keep the pudding from overcooking.) Place in same pan of hot water.
6. Bake in moderate oven (350°) for 10 minutes, or just until peaks turn golden; cool completely, at least 2 hours.
7. Just before serving: Melt remaining apricot and strawberry preserves in separate saucepans over low heat. Strain separately through a sieve; cool slightly. Carefully drizzle apricot preserves and strawberry preserves over meringue.

WINE JELLY WITH FRUITS

Makes 8 servings.

  3 cups water
  1 three-inch piece of stick cinnamon
  3 whole allspice
  1 package (6 ounces) lemon-flavored gelatin
  1 cup dry white wine
  1 can (about 11 ounces) mandarin-orange segments, drained
  1 can (1 pound) purple plums, drained and pitted
  1 can (1 pound) apricot halves, drained
    Maraschino cherries
    Mint leaves

1. Heat water with cinnamon stick and allspice to boiling in a small saucepan; remove spices.
2. Dissolve gelatin in boiling water in a bowl; stir in wine; keep at room temperature.
3. Place an 8-cup mold in a pan of ice and water; pour 1 cup of gelatin mixture into mold and chill until as thick as unbeaten egg white. Arrange mandarin-orange segments in a pattern in gelatin; chill until sticky-firm.
4. Pour 1½ more cups of the room-temperature gelatin into mold and chill until as thick as unbeaten egg white. Arrange purple plums in a pattern in gelatin; chill until sticky-firm.
5. Pour remaining room-temperature gelatin into mold and chill until as thick as unbeaten egg white. Fill the centers of apricot halves with maraschino cherries and arrange in a pattern in gelatin. Chill in refrigerator at least 4 hours.
6. To unmold: Loosen jelly around edges with a knife; dip mold very quickly in and out of a pan of hot water. Wipe water off mold; shake gently to loosen. Cover with plate; turn upside down; lift off mold. Garnish with mint.

CARAMEL CUPS

Bake at 325° for 50 minutes.
Makes 6 servings.

1 cup sugar
6 tablespoons water
2½ cups milk
6 eggs
2 egg yolks
¼ teaspoon salt

1. Combine ½ cup of the sugar and 4 table-spoons of the water in a small heavy saucepan. Heat slowly to boiling, then cook, without stir-ring, just until mixture turns golden. (Watch carefully, for it will caramelize quickly.) Very slowly stir in remaining 2 tablespoons water.
2. Pour about 1 tablespoonful of the hot cara-mel mixture into each of 6 six-ounce custard cups. Tip and turn cups quickly to coat bottom and sides thinly. Let stand while preparing the custard.
3. Heat milk very slowly to scalding in a medi-um-size saucepan.
4. Beat whole eggs and egg yolks slightly in a large bowl; stir in remaining ½ cup sugar and salt; slowly stir in scalded milk. Strain into a 4-cup measure; pour into caramel-coated cups.
5. Set cups in a large pan; place on oven shelf; pour boiling water into pan to within 1 inch of top of cups.
6. Bake in slow oven (325°) 50 minutes, or until center is almost set but still soft. (Do not over-bake; custard will set as it cools.) Remove cups from water; cool. Chill at least 4 hours.
7. To unmold, loosen custards around edges with a small knife; invert onto dessert plates. (Shake cups, if needed, to loosen custards at bottom.) Garnish each with fresh or thawed frozen peach slices, if you wish.

FLOATING ISLAND

Bake at 275° for 25 minutes.
Makes 6 servings.

3 eggs
Dash of salt
6 tablespoons sugar (for meringue)
2 cups milk
¼ cup sugar (for custard)
1 teaspoon vanilla

1. Butter a 6-cup ovenproof mixing bowl or deep baking dish; sprinkle with sugar, then tap out any excess.
2. Separate eggs, placing whites and yolks in separate medium-size bowls.
3. Beat egg whites with salt until foamy-white and double in volume. Sprinkle in the 6 table-spoons sugar, 1 tablespoon at a time, beating all the time until sugar completely dissolves and meringue stands in firm peaks. Spoon the me-ringue into prepared bowl, smoothing carefully against the side.
4. Set bowl in a baking pan; place on oven shelf; pour boiling water into pan to depth of about an inch.
5. Bake in very slow oven (275°) 25 minutes, or until firm and golden. Remove at once from water; cool; chill.
6. While meringue bakes, scald milk slowly in the top of a double boiler over direct heat. Beat egg yolks with the ¼ cup sugar until light and fluffy; very slowly stir in scalded milk; pour back into top of double boiler.
7. Cook, stirring constantly, over simmering water 10 minutes, or until custard thickens slightly and coats spoon; remove from heat. Stir in vanilla; cool; chill.
8. When ready to serve, place several spoonfuls of the custard into a shallow dish. Invert me-ringue into dish, then pour remaining custard around meringue. Garnish with small spoonfuls of your favorite jelly, if you wish. For serving, spoon meringue into dessert dishes, then spoon custard over top.

KITCHEN TIP: HOW TO SEPARATE EGGS

1. To separate an egg, first get out two small bowls. Then, holding the egg in one hand, tap it sharply in the middle with a knife or on the edge of one of the bowls.
2. Hold the egg over one bowl; pull the shell apart and tilt the shell so that the yolk remains in half of shell.
3. Pour yolk back and forth from one half of the shell to the other until all white runs into one bowl. Drop the yolk into the second bowl.
4. To separate more than one egg for a recipe, use two fresh bowls for each egg, following the same 1-2-3 method.

It's beautifully mysterious. The filling may be a luscious layer of fruit or a tangy lemon pudding. You'll never know until you slice into that golden brown crust or scoop past the light meringue topping. Once you do, you're on your way to enjoying one of the best desserts ever—pie. On the next 23 pages we show some of the delicious possibilities for this dessert—without any mysterious preparations! We include recipes for pastries too—those little copycat versions of pies you can pick up in your fingers.

An All-American selection of pies, from left to right, top: Cranberry-Peach Pie, Mincemeat-Pear Pie. Bottom: Rose Chiffon Pie, Macadamia Nut Pie. Recipes are in this chapter.

CHERRY CHEESE PIE

Bake at 350° for 10 minutes.
Makes 1 nine-inch pie.

- **1 package (about 7 ounces) vanilla wafers, crushed**
- **½ cup (1 stick) butter or margarine, melted**
- **1 package (8 ounces) cream cheese, softened**
- **1 can (14 or 15 ounces) sweetened condensed milk**
- **⅓ cup lemon juice**
- **1 teaspoon vanilla**
- **1 can (1 pound, 5 ounces) cherry pie filling**
- **½ teaspoon almond extract**
- **1 cup heavy cream**

1. Blend vanilla-wafer crumbs with melted butter or margarine in a medium-size bowl. Press over bottom and side of a 9-inch pie plate.
2. Bake in moderate oven (350°) 10 minutes, or until set. Cool completely on a wire rack.
3. Beat cream cheese until smooth in a large bowl; slowly beat in condensed milk, then lemon juice and vanilla. Spread evenly in shell.
4. Blend cherry pie filling and almond extract in a medium-size bowl; spoon over cheese filling. Chill at least 3 hours.
5. Just before serving, beat cream until stiff in a medium-size bowl; spoon in a ring around edge on pie.

MACADAMIA NUT PIE

Bake at 325° for 1 hour and 10 minutes.
Makes 1 nine-inch pie.

- **½ package piecrust mix**
- **4 eggs**
- **⅔ cup sugar**
- **¾ cup light corn syrup**
- **¼ cup honey**
- **3 tablespoons butter or margarine, melted and cooled**
- **½ teaspoon vanilla**
- **1¼ cups chopped macadamia nuts**

1. Prepare piecrust mix, following label directions, or make pastry from your favorite single-crust recipe. Roll out to a 12-inch round on a lightly floured pastry cloth or board; fit into a 9-inch pie plate. Trim overhang to ½ inch; turn under, flush with rim; flute for a stand-up edge.

2. Combine eggs, sugar, corn syrup, honey, butter or margarine and vanilla in large bowl of electric mixer; beat about 5 minutes at medium speed, or until light and frothy. Stir in nuts.
3. Pour nut mixture into prepared pastry shell.
4. Bake in slow oven (325°) 1 hour and 10 minutes, or until crust is golden and filling is set at edges but still slightly soft in center. (Do not overbake.) Cool completely on a wire rack. Garnish with whipped cream and additional chopped macadamia nuts, if you wish.

CRANBERRY-PEACH PIE

Bake at 400° for 45 minutes.
Makes 1 nine-inch pie.

- **¾ cup sugar**
- **2 tablespoons flour**
- **1 teaspoon grated lemon rind**
- **¼ teaspoon ground cinnamon**
- **2 cans (about 1 pound each) sliced cling peaches, drained**
- **2 cups fresh cranberries, washed and stemmed**
- **1 package piecrust mix**
- **1 egg, well beaten**
- **½ cup 10X (confectioners') sugar**
- **2 teaspoons water**

1. Mix sugar, flour, lemon rind and cinnamon in a medium-size bowl; add peaches and cranberries. Toss lightly to coat fruit.
2. Prepare piecrust mix, following label directions, or make pastry from your favorite double-crust recipe. Roll out half to a 12-inch round on a lightly floured pastry cloth or board; fit into a 9-inch pie plate; trim overhang to ½ inch. Spoon cranberry-peach mixture into prepared pastry shell.
3. Roll out remaining pastry to an 11-inch round; cut a fancy design or several slits near center to let steam escape; cover pie. Trim overhang to ½ inch; turn edges under, flush with rim; flute to make a stand-up edge.
4. Mix egg with 1 tablespoon water in a bowl; brush over pastry for a rich glaze when baked.
5. Bake in hot oven (400°) 45 minutes, or until top is golden-brown and juices bubble up. Cool on a wire rack.
6. While pie is still warm, mix 10X sugar with water until smooth in bowl. Drizzle over pie.

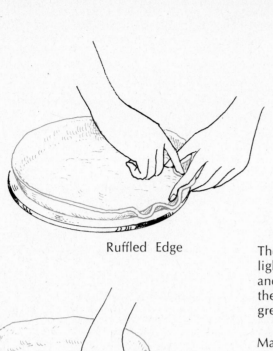

Ruffled Edge

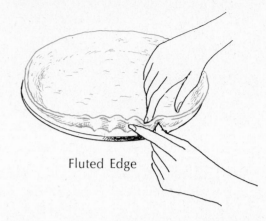

Fluted Edge

The real beauty of any pie lies in its tasty filling and light, flaky crust. But appearance is important, too, and here we show you numerous ways to heighten the eye appeal of your favorite pies—without a great deal of effort.

Make a Fluted Edge: Press right forefinger along inside of rim between thumb and forefinger on outside. Repeat about every inch.

Ruffled Edge: Place left thumb and forefinger about 1/2 inch apart on the inside of rim, and with right forefinger on the outside, pull pastry in.

Rope Edge: Twisting slightly, press a slim pencil (or wooden skewer) diagonally into pastry all around edge to make even, widely spaced ridges.

For a Lattice Top to Use on Cherry Pie: Cut pastry strips from leftover piecrust dough. Lay half the strips evenly across top of filled pie. Handle carefully to avoid stretching or tearing dough. Then weave the first cross strip, over and under, through center. Each time you add another strip, fold back every other right-angle strip.

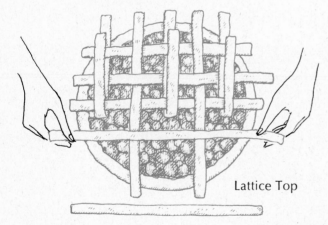

Rope Edge

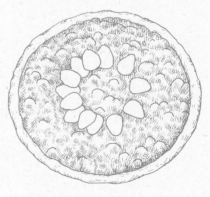

Lattice Top

Cream Cheese Petals

Decorative Piecrusts and Trims

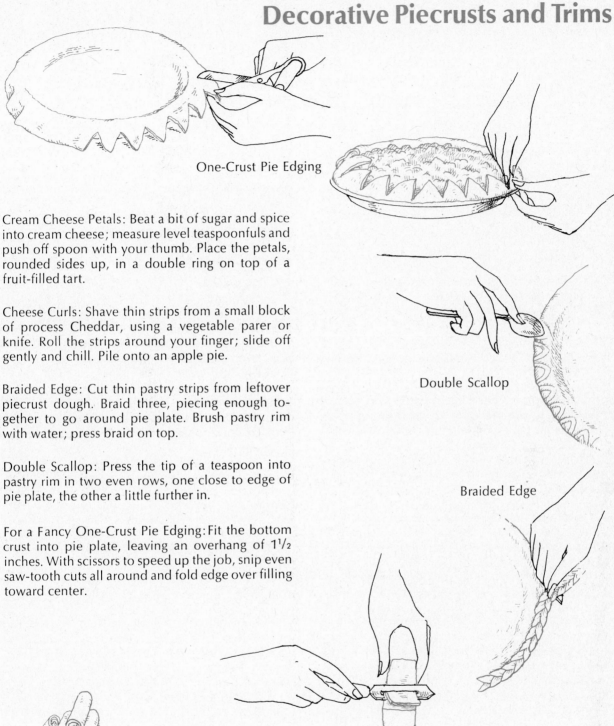

One-Crust Pie Edging

Cream Cheese Petals: Beat a bit of sugar and spice into cream cheese; measure level teaspoonfuls and push off spoon with your thumb. Place the petals, rounded sides up, in a double ring on top of a fruit-filled tart.

Cheese Curls: Shave thin strips from a small block of process Cheddar, using a vegetable parer or knife. Roll the strips around your finger; slide off gently and chill. Pile onto an apple pie.

Braided Edge: Cut thin pastry strips from leftover piecrust dough. Braid three, piecing enough together to go around pie plate. Brush pastry rim with water; press braid on top.

Double Scallop: Press the tip of a teaspoon into pastry rim in two even rows, one close to edge of pie plate, the other a little further in.

For a Fancy One-Crust Pie Edging: Fit the bottom crust into pie plate, leaving an overhang of $1\frac{1}{2}$ inches. With scissors to speed up the job, snip even saw-tooth cuts all around and fold edge over filling toward center.

Double Scallop

Braided Edge

Cheese Curls

LEMON MERINGUE PIE

Bake the shell in a 450° oven for 8 to 10 minutes. Bake the meringue puffs at 425° for 3 to 5 minutes.
Makes 1 eight-inch pie.

½ **package piecrust mix**
1 ⅓ **cups sugar (for filling)**
⅓ **cup cornstarch**
¼ **teaspoon salt**
1 ¾ **cups water**
4 **eggs, separated**
2 **tablespoons butter or margarine**
1 **tablespoon grated lemon rind**
½ **cup lemon juice (about 4 lemons)**
¼ **teaspoon cream of tartar**
½ **cup sugar (for meringue)**

1. Prepare piecrust mix, following label directions, or make pastry from your favorite single-crust recipe. Roll out to a 10-inch round on a lightly floured pastry board; fit into an 8-inch pie plate. Trim overhang to ½ inch; turn under, flush with rim. Flute edge or scallop the edge with an inverted teaspoon, pressing down hard for each cut to form design.
2. Bake in hot oven (450°) 8 to 10 minutes, or until golden brown; cool.
3. Combine 1⅓ cups sugar, cornstarch and salt in a medium-size pan; gradually stir in water.
4. Cook over medium heat, stirring constantly, until mixture comes to boiling and is thickened. Boil 1 minute. Remove from heat.
5. Beat egg yolks slightly in a small bowl; slowly blend in about ½ cup of the hot cornstarch mixture; slowly stir back into remaining mixture in saucepan. Cook, stirring constantly, over low heat 2 minutes; remove from heat. (Do not overcook.) Stir in butter or margarine, lemon rind and lemon juice; pour into cooled pastry shell. Cover with plastic wrap; refrigerate until cold, about 3 hours.
6. Beat egg whites with cream of tartar until foamy-white and double in volume in a medium-size bowl; sprinkle in remaining ½ cup sugar, 1 tablespoon at a time, beating all the time until sugar dissolves completely and meringue stands in firm peaks.
7. Using a pastry bag with a large notched tip, press meringue into 10 to 12 large puffs on a greased and lightly floured cooky sheet. If you do not have a pastry bag, you can spoon the meringue into puffs on a floured cooky sheet.
8. Bake in hot oven (425°) 3 to 5 minutes, or just until peaks turn golden. Cool on cooky sheet. When the puffs are cool, carefully place on the cold pie with a small spatula. Garnish with lemon slices, if you wish.

BLACK BOTTOM PIE

Bake shell at 400° for 15 minutes.
Makes 1 nine-inch pie.

½ **package piecrust mix**
2 **tablespoons cornstarch**
1 ¼ **cups sugar**
3 **cups milk**
6 **egg yolks, well beaten**
1 ½ **teaspoons vanilla**
2 **squares unsweetened chocolate, melted**
1 **envelope unflavored gelatin**
¼ **cup cold water**
3 **tablespoons rum**
4 **egg whites**

1. Prepare piecrust mix, following label directions, or make pastry from your favorite single-crust recipe. Roll out to a 12-inch round on a lightly floured pastry board; fit into a 9-inch pie plate. Trim overhang to ½ inch; turn under, flush with rim; flute to make a stand-up edge. Prick shell well with a fork.
2. Bake in hot oven (400°) 15 minutes, or until pastry is golden. Cool completely in pie plate on a wire rack.
3. Combine cornstarch and ¾ cup of the sugar in a medium-size saucepan: stir in milk slowly. Cook over low heat, stirring constantly until thickened. Blend a small amount of the hot mixture into beaten egg yolks; add to hot mixture in saucepan. Cook 2 minutes longer, stirring constantly, until custard coats spoon. Remove from heat; stir in vanilla.
4. Measure out 2 cups of the custard into a medium-size bowl; stir in chocolate; cool. Pour into baked pastry shell. Chill.
5. Soften gelatin in water in a custard cup; add to remaining hot custard; stir until dissolved. Stir in rum. Place bowl in a larger bowl partly filled with ice and water to speed setting. Chill, stirring often, until slightly thickened.
6. Beat egg whites until foamy-white and double in volume in a medium-size bowl; beat in

remaining ½ cup sugar, 1 tablespoon at a time, until meringue stands in firm peaks.

7. Fold meringue into chilled gelatin mixture; chill again just until mixture mounds. Spoon over chocolate layer.

8. Chill several hours, preferably overnight, until firm. Garnish with whipped cream and chocolate sprinkles, if you wish.

PINWHEEL PUMPKIN PIE

Bake at 425° for 15 minutes, then at 350° for 35 minutes.
Makes 1 nine-inch pie.

    ½ package piecrust mix
     2 eggs
     1 can (1 pound) pumpkin
    ½ cup granulated sugar
    ½ cup firmly packed brown sugar
     1 teaspoon ground cinnamon
    ¼ teaspoon ground cloves
    ¼ teaspoon ground nutmeg
     1 teaspoon salt
     1 tall can evaporated milk
     1 can (1 pound, 13 ounces) sliced cling peaches
     1 jar (12 ounces) peach preserves

1. Prepare piecrust mix, following label directions, or make pastry from your favorite single-crust recipe. Roll out to a 12-inch round on a lightly floured pastry board; fit into a 9-inch pie plate. Trim overhang to ½ inch; turn under, flush with rim; flute to make a stand-up edge.

2. Beat eggs slightly in a large bowl; stir in pumpkin, granulated and brown sugars, cinnamon, cloves, nutmeg, salt and evaporated milk. Pour into prepared pastry shell.

3. Bake in hot oven (425°) 15 minutes. Lower oven temperature to moderate (350°); continue baking 35 minutes, or until custard is almost set but still soft in center. (Do not overbake; custard will set as it cools.) Cool pie completely on a wire rack.

4. Drain syrup from peach slices; pat fruit dry with paper toweling.

5. Heat preserves until hot in a small saucepan; press through a sieve into a small bowl. Holding each peach slice on a fork, dip into preserves, then arrange in a ring around edge on pie. Chill the pie well until serving time.

PARISIENNE FRUIT TART

Bake at 400° for 20 minutes.
Makes 8 servings.

     1 package (10 ounces) frozen patty shells
        Sugar
     1 cup milk
     1 cup heavy cream
     1 package (4 ounces) vanilla-flavor soft dessert mix
     2 medium-size bananas
     2 tablespoons lemon juice
    ⅓ cup apricot preserves
     2 cups seedless green grapes, washed (¾ pound)
     1 can (8¼ ounces) sliced pineapple, drained

1. Remove patty shells from package. Thaw at room temperature one half hour.

2. Place rounds of pastry, overlapping slightly, lengthwise on a lightly floured surface. Roll to a 16x4-inch rectangle. (If patties separate, moisten with a few drops of water.) Place on an ungreased large cooky sheet; trim edges evenly; prick well with fork; chill 30 minutes.

3. Reroll trimmings thinly; cut into ⅓-inch-wide strips about 4 inches long; brush with water; press ends together to make rings. Brush rings with water, then dip in sugar; place on cooky sheet along with rectangle of pastry. Bake pastry and pastry rings in hot oven (400°) 10 minutes. Remove rings to wire rack; reserve for decoration. Bake pastry rectangle 10 minutes longer, or until golden-brown. Remove to rack; cool.

4. Combine milk, ¼ cup of the cream and dessert mix in a small deep bowl; beat, following label directions. Chill 15 minutes. Peel and cut bananas into ¼-inch-thick slices. Sprinkle with half the lemon juice.

5. Split pastry into two layers. Place bottom layer on long serving dish or board; spread with about ⅔ of soft dessert; arrange banana slices on long side edges; spread with remaining dessert mix. Top with second pastry layer. Heat apricot preserves with remaining lemon juice until melted in small saucepan; cool slightly. Brush all over tart.

6. Beat remaining cream until stiff in a small bowl; spread over top of pastry. Arrange rows of grapes in cream, starting at outer edges. Cut pineapple slices in half and place in center. Complete the garnish with reserved pastry rings.

WALNUT PIE

Bake at 375° for 40 minutes.
Makes 6 servings.

½ cup butter or margarine, at room
  temperature
1 cup firmly packed dark brown sugar
1 cup dark corn syrup
4 eggs, lightly beaten
  Pinch of salt
1 teaspoon vanilla
1 unbaked eight-inch or nine-inch pie shell
1 cup coarsely chopped walnuts

1. Preheat the oven to 375°.
2. Cream together the butter or margarine and brown sugar in a mixing bowl. Blend in the syrup. Beat in the eggs.
3. Add the salt and vanilla to the mixture and pour into the pie shell. Sprinkle walnuts over the top.
4. Bake 40 minutes, or until filling is firm.

NECTARINE RASPBERRY TURNOVERS

Bake at 375° for 25 minutes.
Makes 12 turnovers.

Sour-Cream Pastry:
3 cups sifted all-purpose flour
2 tablespoons sugar
1 cup (2 sticks) butter or margarine
1 cup dairy sour cream
Filling:
¼ cup sugar
1 cup peeled, pitted and thinly sliced nectarines (about ½ pound)
1 package (10 ounces) quick thaw frozen raspberries, thawed and drained
  Water
  Sugar

1. Make Sour-Cream Pastry—Measure flour and sugar into a medium-size bowl. Cut in butter or margarine with a pastry blender until mixture is crumbly; add sour cream. Mix lightly with a fork until dough clings together and starts to leave sides of bowl. Gather dough together with hands and knead a few times. Wrap dough in wax paper; chill several hours, or overnight.
2. Make Filling just before baking—Sprinkle sugar over nectarines in a small bowl; toss with a fork to mix well; add the well-drained raspberries. Preheat oven to hot (400°).
3. Divide dough in half. Keep one half refrigerated until ready to use. Roll out other half to a 15x10-inch rectangle; trim edges even with pastry wheel or sharp knife. Cut into six 5-inch squares. Place about 2 tablespoons filling on each square; moisten edges with water; fold over to make a triangle. Crimp edges with a fork to seal. Lift onto ungreased cooky sheet.
4. Reroll trimmings; cut into small leaves and rounds with a truffle cutter or pastry wheel. Brush tops of pastries with water; decorate with pastry cutouts; make 1 or 2 small gashes in top of each triangle to let steam escape. Sprinkle each turnover with sugar.
5. Lower oven temperature to moderate (375°) as soon as you put turnovers in. Bake 25 minutes, or until puffed and rich brown in color; remove to wire rack to cool. Serve warm. Repeat with remaining pastry and filling.
NOTE: If you wish to bake only 6 turnovers, shape and fill second half of pastry. Place in a single layer on a cooky sheet; freeze. When frozen, wrap in foil or transparent wrap. When ready to use, bake as directed, increasing baking time by about 5 minutes. There is no need to defrost.

GLAZED APPLE CHEESE PIE

Makes 6 servings.

1 three-ounce package cream cheese
1 tablespoon milk or dairy sour cream
1 baked nine-inch pie shell
6 large apples that hold their shape as they cook, such as Rome or Delicious
1½ cups plus two tablespoons water
1 cup sugar
1 three-inch piece stick cinnamon
1 teaspoon grated lemon rind
2 tablespoons lemon juice
2 tablespoons cornstarch
  Red food coloring

1. Soften the cream cheese with the milk or sour cream and spread over the bottom of the pie shell.
2. Peel the apples and cut into eighths. Place 1½ cups of the water and the sugar in a saucepan and bring to a boil. Drop in the apple

pieces and cinnamon stick and simmer until apples are barely tender but not broken.

3. With a slotted spoon, remove apple pieces. Drain and let cool. Discard cinnamon stick. Measure 1¼ cups of the apple syrup.

4. Add the lemon rind and lemon juice to apple syrup. Mix together the cornstarch and remaining water. Stir into apple syrup mixture. Bring to a boil, stirring, and cook two minutes over very low heat, stirring constantly. Color faintly pink with food coloring.

5. Fill the pie shell with the apple pieces, arranging the top layer in an attractive pattern. Spoon glaze over the apples. Serve at room temperature. Garnish with whipped cream, if you wish.

UPSIDE DOWN PEAR TART

Bake at 425° for 30 minutes.
Makes 8 servings.

7 firm, ripe pears (about 3½ pounds)
¾ cup sugar
½ cup (1 stick) butter or margarine
½ package piecrust mix
½ cup heavy cream, whipped

1. Pare, halve and core pears. Slice 7 or 8 halves crosswise and on an angle, each into 4 or 5 slices, keeping slices intact. Arrange as whole halves in a 9-inch-deep pie plate, rounded side down and stem ends toward center; trim one pear half to a round to fit center. Slice remaining pears into ½-inch slices; arrange on top to fill plate.

2. Melt ½ cup of the sugar over medium-high heat in a small heavy skillet; continue heating until sugar caramelizes and turns golden-brown. Remove from heat; quickly stir in butter or margarine until almost melted, then pour over pears.

3. Prepare piecrust mix, following label directions or make pastry from your favorite single-crust recipe. Roll out to a 10-inch round on a lightly floured pastry board; place on top of pears. Do not attach to edge.

4. Bake in hot oven (425°) for 30 minutes, or until crust is golden and pears are done. (Place a piece of foil under pie in case juices should bubble out.) Cool on wire rack about 30 minutes. Invert onto a serving platter with a rim.

(Pie will have formed a syrup.) With a baster or spoon, remove syrup to a 1-cup measure. (You should then have about ¾ cup, depending on the fruit.)

5. Melt remaining ¼ cup sugar in a small heavy saucepan. Heat very slowly until sugar melts into a colorless liquid, then turns golden-brown color and is caramelized. Stir in the reserved fruit syrup from the tart. Boil the syrup rapidly until it is reduced to about ½ cup. It will be slightly thickened. Take care it does not scorch as you are boiling.

6. Just before serving, spoon warm caramel sauce evenly over tart, reserving one tablespoon. Spoon whipped cream onto center; drizzle reserved caramel sauce over.

LEMON BLOSSOM TART

Bake shell at 400° for 20 minutes.
Makes 8 servings.

1 package piecrust mix
2 tablespoons sugar (for pastry)
4 eggs
½ cup sugar (for filling)
2 teaspoons grated lemon rind
¼ cup lemon juice
4 tablespoons (½ stick) butter or margarine
1 cup heavy cream

1. Combine piecrust mix, the 2 tablespoons sugar and 1 of the eggs in a medium-size bowl. Mix with a fork until well-blended.

2. Press evenly over bottom and up side of a 9x1½-inch layer-cake pan, making rim even with edge of pan. (Shell will be thicker than standard piecrust.) Prick well all over with a fork.

3. Bake in hot oven (400°) 20 minutes, or until golden. Cool completely in pan on a wire rack.

4. Beat remaining 3 eggs slightly in the top of a double boiler; stir in the ½ cup sugar, lemon rind and juice, and butter or margarine. Cook, stirring constantly, over hot (not boiling) water 10 minutes, or until very thick. Pour into a medium-size bowl; chill until completely cold.

5. Beat cream until stiff in a medium-size bowl; fold into lemon custard.

6. Remove pastry shell carefully from pan; place on a large serving plate; spoon lemon filling into shell. Garnish with additional whipped cream, if you wish. Chill 1 hour before serving.

BLACKBERRY PINEAPPLE TURNOVERS

Bake at 375° for 25 minutes.
Makes 12 turnovers.

1 can (8 ounces) pineapple tidbits
1 tablespoon cornstarch
2 tablespoons sugar
  Dash ground nutmeg
  Dash ground cloves
2 cups fresh or frozen blackberries
1 recipe Sour-Cream Pastry (page 68)

1. Drain pineapple into a 1-cup measure; add water to make ½ cup. Combine with cornstarch, sugar, nutmeg and cloves in a small saucepan; mix well.
2. Stir in blackberries. Bring to boiling, stirring constantly; bubble 1 minute. Remove from heat, stir in pineapple. Cool.
3. Make Sour-Cream Pastry; fill and bake turnovers, following directions for Nectarine Raspberry Turnovers (page 68).

CIDER APPLE PIE

Bake at 425° for 25 minutes.
Makes 6 servings.

½ pound dried apples
3 cups cider
½ cup sugar
½ teaspoon ground cinnamon
¼ teaspoon ground nutmeg
  Pastry for a two-crust nine-inch pie
2 tablespoons butter or margarine

1. Place the apples and cider in a saucepan. Bring to a boil and simmer until apples are tender and plump.
2. Combine the sugar, cinnamon and nutmeg; add to apples and cook 10 minutes longer. The apples should have absorbed most of the juice. Cool slightly.
3. Preheat the oven to 425°.
4. Line a 9-inch pie plate with half the pastry. Pour in the apple filling. Roll remaining pastry into a rectangle and cut into ½-inch strips. Dot apple mixture with butter or margarine and make a lattice of pastry.
5. Bake 25 minutes, or until filling is bubbly and pastry is golden brown. Remove from oven; serve warm. Or, let the pie cool completely.

DEVONSHIRE APPLE PIE

Bake at 350° for 40 minutes.
Makes 1 nine-inch pie.

¾ cup granulated sugar
¼ cup firmly packed brown sugar
1 tablespoon flour
½ teaspoon ground cinnamon
¼ teaspoon ground nutmeg
1 teaspoon lemon juice
⅛ teaspoon salt
½ cup dairy sour cream
4 medium-size apples, pared, quartered, cored and sliced (4 cups)
1 nine-inch unbaked pastry shell
  Streusel Topping (recipe follows)

1. Mix granulated and brown sugars, flour, spices, lemon juice and salt in a large bowl; stir in sour cream and apples. Spoon into pastry shell; sprinkle with Streusel Topping.
2. Bake in moderate oven (350°) 40 minutes, or until apples are tender and topping is golden. Cool.
3. Just before serving, garnish with Cheddar cheese slices, if you wish.

STREUSEL TOPPING: Mix ½ cup flour and ½ cup firmly packed brown sugar in a small bowl. Cut in 4 tablespoons (½ stick) butter or margarine with pastry blender until crumbly.

DOUBLE APPLE TURNOVERS

Bake at 375° for 25 minutes.
Makes 12 turnovers.

2 cups chopped, pared apples (2 small)
¾ cup applesauce
¼ cup firmly packed light brown sugar
½ teaspoon ground cinnamon
¼ teaspoon ground mace
2 tablespoons raisins
1 recipe Sour-Cream Pastry (page 68)

1. Combine apples, applesauce, sugar, cinnamon, mace and raisins in a small bowl. Mix well with a fork.
2. Make Sour-Cream Pastry; fill and bake turnovers, following directions for Nectarine Raspberry Turnovers. (The recipe is on page 68).

Right: Great apple desserts include Sugar-Frosted Apple Pie (far right), Glazed Apple Jalousie and Meringue Apples (top). Recipes for pie and Jalousie in this chapter. Meringue recipe is in Chapter 8.

COCONUT CREAM PIE

Bake shell at 425° for 15 minutes.
Makes 1 nine-inch pie.

½ **package piecrust mix**
⅔ **cup sugar**
¼ **cup cornstarch**
3 **tablespoons flour**
½ **teaspoon salt**
2½ **cups milk**
2 **eggs**
2 **tablespoons butter or margarine**
1 **teaspoon vanilla**
1½ **cups heavy cream**
1 **cup grated fresh coconut**
 OR: 1 can (about 4 ounces) flaked coconut
½ **cup apricot preserves**

1. Prepare piecrust mix, following label directions, or make pastry from your own single-crust recipe.
2. Roll out to 12-inch round on a lightly floured pastry board; fit into a 9-inch pie plate. Trim overhang to ½ inch; turn under, flush with rim; flute edge. Prick shell well with a fork.
3. Bake in hot oven (425°) 15 minutes, or until golden; cool.
4. Mix sugar, cornstarch, flour and salt in the top of a double boiler; stir in milk. Cook over simmering water, stirring constantly, until mixture thickens; cover. Cook 15 minutes longer; remove from heat.
5. Beat eggs slightly in a small bowl; slowly stir in about half of the hot mixture; stir back into remaining mixture in double boiler. Cook over simmering water, stirring constantly, 3 minutes; remove from heat. Stir in butter or margarine and the vanilla. Pour into a medium-size bowl; cover surface with wax paper or transparent wrap; chill.
6. Beat ½ cup of the cream until stiff in a small bowl. Fold the 1 cup grated (or 1 cup flaked) coconut into chilled pudding, then fold in whipped cream.
7. Whip ½ cup of the apricot preserves until soft in a small bowl; spread in cooled pastry shell; spoon cream filling on top. Chill at least 2 hours, or until firm enough to cut.
8. Just before serving, beat cream until stiff in a small bowl. Spread decoratively on top of pie; garnish with shredded coconut or rest of flaked coconut. Slice and serve.

LEMON TARTLETS VERONIQUE

Bake shells at 375° for 22 minutes.
Makes 1 dozen.

2 **cups sifted all-purpose flour**
3 **tablespoons sugar**
½ **teaspoon salt**
½ **cup (1 stick) butter or margarine**
¼ **cup shortening**
6 **tablespoons water**
 Lemon Filling (recipe follows)
1 **pound seedless green grapes, stemmed and halved**
1 **cup apple jelly, melted and cooled**
1 **cup heavy cream**

1. Sift flour, sugar and salt into a medium-size bowl. Cut in butter or margarine and shortening with a pastry blender until mixture is crumbly.
2. Sprinkle water over top; mix lightly with a fork until pastry holds together and leaves side of bowl clean. Turn out onto a lightly floured pastry board; knead just until smooth; divide into 12 even pieces. Chill dough at least an hour for easier handling.
3. Press each piece of dough into a fluted 3-inch tart-shell pan to cover bottom and side evenly. Fit a small piece of wax paper over pastry in each pan; pour uncooked rice or beans on top to hold pastry in place during baking. Set tart-shell pans in a large shallow pan.
4. Bake in moderate oven (375°) 10 minutes; remove from oven. Lift out wax paper and rice or beans; return pans to oven. Bake 12 minutes longer, or until pastry is golden. Cool shells completely in pans on wire racks, then remove carefully from pans.
5. Spoon Lemon Filling into each shell; arrange grape halves, cut sides up, on top to form rosettes; brush grapes with apply jelly; chill.
6. Just before serving, beat cream until stiff in a medium-size bowl. Attach a fancy tip to a pastry bag; fill bag with whipped cream; decorate tops of tarts. Chill until serving time.

LEMON FILLING: Beat 6 eggs slightly in the top of a large double boiler; stir in 1 cup sugar, ½ cup (1 stick) butter or margarine, 2 teaspoons grated lemon rind and ⅓ cup lemon juice. Cook, stirring constantly, over hot, not boiling, water 15 minutes, or until very thick. Pour into a medium-size bowl; cover, chill. Makes 3 cups.

Left, starting from top: Walnut Pie, Glazed Apple Cheese Pie and Cider Apple Pie. On pages 72-73, from left to right: Parisienne Fruit Tart, Upside-Down Pear Tart and Fresh Fruit Tarts (far right).

TART A L'ORANGE

Bake at 400° for 35 minutes.
Makes 8 servings.

1 package (12 ounces) frozen patty shells, thawed
6 medium-size oranges
4 egg yolks
⅓ cup sugar
¼ cup flour
1 teaspoon grated lemon rind
6 ladyfingers
½ cup apricot preserves
1 tablespoon sugar
6 tablespoons Grand Marnier

1. Heat oven to very hot (450°).
2. Arrange patty shells in circle, just touching, on a floured pastry board. Roll out, keeping circular shape, to a 12-inch round. Fit into a 9-inch layer-cake pan with removable bottom or a 9-inch fluted quiche pan. Turn edge under; crimp. Fit a piece of foil into shell; fill shell with beans or rice.
3. Put shell into preheated oven; immediately turn heat down to 400°. Bake shell 15 minutes; remove beans and paper. Sprinkle bottom with sugar; prick lightly with a fork. Bake 20 minutes longer, or until golden and crisp and sugar is starting to caramelize. Cool on wire rack.
4. Grate 1 orange; reserve the rind. Squeeze enough oranges to yield 1½ cups.
5. Beat egg yolks slightly in top of double boiler. Beat in sugar and flour; stir in orange juice. Cook over hot, not boiling water, until very thick, about 7 minutes, or until mixture mounds when dropped from spoon; cool. Add orange and lemon rinds.
6. Split ladyfingers in half. Slice each half lengthwise in half again.
7. Simmer apricot preserves and the 1 tablespoon sugar with 2 tablespoons of the Grand Marnier in a small saucepan 2 minutes; rub through a fine sieve; cool slightly.
8. Slice the two remaining oranges in paper-thin slices; remove any seeds. (Notch edges, if you wish.) Put on a large plate; sprinkle with remaining 4 tablespoons Grand Marnier. Let stand 10 minutes.
9. Spoon orange cream into shell. Arrange the thin slices of ladyfingers over cream to cover completely (a chef's secret to absorb excess juice from orange slices). Fill in spaces with pieces cut to fit. Drain oranges. Sprinkle ladyfingers with liqueur drained from oranges.
10. Arrange orange slices over ladyfingers, slightly overlapping, in a circular pattern. Brush oranges and pastry with the preserves. Cool slightly. Refrigerate, unless serving at once.

CHOCOLATE-NUT CREAM PIE

Bake shell at 400° for 15 minutes.
Makes 1 nine-inch pie.

½ package piecrust mix
¾ cup sugar
1 envelope unflavored gelatin
2 teaspoons cornstarch
3 eggs, separated
1 cup milk
¼ cup light rum
¼ teaspoon cream of tartar
1 cup heavy cream

1. Prepare piecrust mix, following label directions, or make pastry from your favorite single-crust recipe. Roll out to a 12-inch round on a lightly floured pastry board; fit into a 9-inch pie plate. Trim overhang to ½ inch; turn under, flush with rim; flute to make a stand-up edge. Prick shell well all over with a fork.
2. Bake in hot oven (400°) 15 minutes, or until pastry is golden. Cool completely in pie plate on a wire rack.
3. Mix ½ cup of the sugar, gelatin and cornstarch in a medium-size saucepan; beat in egg yolks and milk. Cook over low heat, stirring constantly, until gelatin dissolves and mixture coats spoon; pour into a large bowl; stir in rum.
4. Place bowl in a pan of ice and water to speed setting; chill, stirring several times, just until as thick as unbeaten egg white.
5. While gelatin mixture chills, beat egg whites with cream of tartar until foamy-white in a medium-size bowl; beat in remaining ¼ cup sugar, 1 tablespoon at a time, until meringue stands in firm peaks. Beat cream until stiff in a small bowl.
6. Fold meringue, then whipped cream into thickened gelatin mixture until no streaks of white remain; spoon into cooled pastry shell. Chill at least three hours, or until firm. Just before serving, garnish with more whipped cream.

BANANA CREAM PIE

Makes 1 nine-inch pie.

¼ **cup cornstarch**
⅔ **cup sugar**
¼ **teaspoon salt**
2 **cups milk**
2 **eggs, slightly beaten**
2 **tablespoons butter or margarine**
½ **teaspoon vanilla**
2 **large bananas**
1 **nine-inch baked pastry shell**
½ **cup heavy cream, whipped**

1. Mix cornstarch, sugar and salt in a medium-size saucepan. Add milk. Cook over moderate heat, stirring constantly, until mixture thickens and boils. Cook 1 minute longer.
2. Stir small amount of hot mixture into egg in a small bowl; mix well. Stir rapidly into hot mixture in pan; cook 1 minute, stirring constantly. Add butter or margarine and vanilla; cool slightly.
3. Slice bananas over bottom of pie shell; pour filling over bananas. Refrigerate about 2 hours, or until firm. Garnish with whipped cream.

NECTARINE PIE

Bake at 425° for 45 minutes.
Makes 1 nine-inch pie.

1 **package piecrust mix**
4 **cups sliced pared nectarines**
½ **cup granulated sugar**
¼ **cup firmly packed brown sugar**
¼ **cup flour**
1 **teaspoon grated lemon rind**
¼ **teaspoon ground cinnamon**
⅛ **teaspon salt**
1 **teaspoon lemon juice**
2 **tablespoons butter or margarine**
1 **tablespoon milk or cream**

1. Prepare piecrust mix, following label directions, or make pastry from your own favorite two-crust recipe. Roll out half to a 12-inch round on a lightly floured pastry cloth or board; fit into a 9-inch pie plate; trim any overhang to about ½ inch.
2. Place nectarines in a large bowl. Sprinkle with granulated and brown sugars, flour, lemon rind, cinnamon, salt and lemon juice; toss lightly to mix. Spoon into prepared pastry shell; dot with butter or margarine.
3. Roll out remaining pastry to an 11-inch round; cut several small designs in crust with a knife; remove cutouts; place crust over pie. Trim overhang to ½ inch; turn edges under, flush with rim; flute edge all around. Brush top with milk or cream.
4. Bake in hot oven (425°) 45 minutes, or until pastry is golden and juices bubble up. Cool pie on a wire rack. Serve plain or with cream.

CINNAMON-APPLE PIE

Bake at 400° for 35 minutes.
Makes 1 nine-inch pie.

2 **cans (1 pound, 4 ounces each) pie-sliced apples**
⅔ **cup sugar (for filling)**
¼ **cup cornstarch**
¼ **cup red-hot cinnamon candies**
2 **tablespoons butter or margarine**
1 **package piecrust mix**
   Milk
   Sugar (for topping)

1. Drain liquid from apples into a cup; place apples in a large bowl.
2. Mix ⅓ cup of the sugar and cornstarch in a small saucepan; stir in ⅓ cup of the apple liquid, cinnamon candies and butter or margarine. Cook slowly, stirring constantly, until candies melt and mixture thickens and boils 3 minutes. Stir in remaining ⅓ cup sugar; pour over apples; cool.
3. Prepare piecrust mix, following label directions, or make pastry from your favorite double-crust recipe. Roll out half to a 12-inch round on a lightly floured pastry board; fit into a 9-inch pie plate. Trim overhang to ½ inch. Spoon apple mixture into crust.
4. Roll out remaining pastry to an 11-inch round; place over filling; cut vents in pastry for steam to escape. Trim overhang to ½ inch; turn edge under, flush with rim; flute to make a standup edge. Brush top crust with milk; sprinkle with sugar.
5. Bake in hot oven (400°) 35 minutes, or until pastry is golden. Cool pie completely on a rack.

PUMPKIN PARTY TARTS

Makes 12 three-inch tarts.

- **1 envelope unflavored gelatin**
- **½ cup sugar**
- **1 can (1 pound) pumpkin**
- **½ teaspoon ground cinnamon**
- **¼ teaspoon ground ginger**
- **¼ teaspoon ground cloves**
- **¼ cup orange juice**
- **1 pint vanilla ice cream**
- **12 baked 3-inch tart shells**
- **Whipped cream**
- **Pecans**

1. Combine gelatin and sugar in a medium-size saucepan. Stir in pumpkin, cinnamon, ginger, cloves and orange juice.
2. Cook, stirring constantly, until mixture bubbles and gelatin dissolves. Remove from heat and add ice cream, a few spoonfuls at a time.
3. Spoon pumpkin mixture into baked tart shells. Chill 4 hours, or overnight.
4. Party time: Swirl whipped cream onto the top of each tart and garnish with whole pecans.

HARVEST PECAN PIE

Bake at 425° for 10 minutes, then at 350° for 30 minutes.
Makes 1 nine-inch pie.

- **½ package piecrust mix**
- **2 cups pecans**
- **½ cup (1 stick) butter or margarine**
- **1 cup sugar**
- **4 eggs**
- **½ cup dairy sour cream**
- **2 teaspoons grated lemon rind**
- **1 cup chopped pitted dates**
- **1 cup seedless raisins**

1. Prepare piecrust mix, following label directions, or make pastry from your favorite single-crust recipe. Roll out to a 12-inch round on a lightly floured pastry board; fit into a 9-inch pie plate. Trim overhang to ½ inch; turn under, flush with rim; flute to make a stand-up edge.
2. Set aside ½ cup of the pecans for topping, then chop remainder coarsely.
3. Cream butter or margarine with sugar until fluffy in a large bowl; beat in eggs, one at a time, until well-blended. Stir in sour cream, lemon rind, the chopped pecans, dates and raisins. Spoon into prepared pastry shell; arrange remaining pecans over filling.
4. Bake in hot oven (425°) 10 minutes. Lower oven temperature to moderate (350°); continue baking 30 minutes, or until filling is set. Cool pie completely on a wire rack.

BRANDIED CHOCOLATE PIE

Bake shell at 275° for 1 hour.
Makes 1 nine-inch pie.

- **4 egg whites**
- **¼ teaspoon cream of tartar**
- **¼ teaspon salt**
- **½ teaspoon vanilla**
- **1 cup sugar**
- **½ cup maraschino cherries, drained and quartered**
- **2 tablespoons brandy**
- **2 envelopes unflavored gelatin**
- **¾ cup water**
- **2 pints chocolate ice cream**
- **½ cup heavy cream**

1. Generously butter a 9-inch pie plate.
2. Beat egg whites with cream of tartar, salt and vanilla until foamy-white and double in volume in a large bowl. With electric mixer, beat in sugar, 1 tablespoon at a time, beating all the time until sugar dissolves completely and meringue stands in firm peaks.
3. Spoon meringue into pie plate; spread almost to side of plate, hollowing center and building up edge slightly to form a shell.
4. Bake in very slow oven (275°) 1 hour, or until firm and lightly golden. Cool completely in pie plate on a wire rack.
5. Combine cherries with brandy in a small bowl; let stand to season.
6. Soften gelatin in water in a medium-size saucepan; heat slowly, stirring constantly, until gelatin dissolves; pour into a large bowl. Stir in cherry mixture, then beat in ice cream, a few spoonfuls at a time; pour into meringue shell. Chill several hours, or until firm.
7. Just before serving, beat cream in a small bowl until stiff. Spread over top of pie. Garnish the pie with additional cherries, if you wish.

VIRGINIA PECAN PIE

Bake at 350° for 45 minutes.
Makes 1 nine-inch pie.

- ½ **package piecrust mix**
- 4 **eggs**
- 1 **cup sugar**
- ½ **teaspoon salt**
- 1½ **cups dark corn syrup**
- 1 **teaspoon vanilla**
- ¼ **cup all-purpose flour**
- 1 **cup pecan halves**

1. Prepare piecrust mix, following label directions, or make pastry from your favorite single-crust recipe. Roll out to a 12-inch round on a lightly floured board; fit into a 9-inch pie plate. Trim overhang flush with rim. Press pastry to rim with the tines of a fork.
2. Beat eggs slightly in a medium-size bowl; blend in sugar, salt, corn syrup and vanilla; stir in flour. Pour into prepared shell; arrange pecan halves in pattern on top.
3. Bake in moderate oven (350°) 45 minutes, or until center is almost set but still soft. (Do not overbake, for filling will set as it cools.) Cool on wire rack. Serve with whipped cream.

ORANGE CHIFFON PIE

Bake shell at 425° for 15 minutes.
Makes 1 eight-inch pie.

- ½ **package piecrust mix**
- 4 **eggs, separated**
- 1 **cup sugar**
- ¼ **teaspoon salt**
- ¾ **cup orange juice**
- 1 **envelope unflavored gelatin**
- ¼ **teaspoon cream of tartar**
- ½ **cup heavy cream**

1. Prepare piecrust mix, following label directions, or make your favorite one-crust recipe. Roll out to an 11-inch round on a lightly floured pastry board; fit into an 8-inch pie plate. Trim overhang to ½ inch; turn edge under, flush with rim; flute to make a stand-up edge. Prick shell well all over with a fork.
2. Bake in hot oven (425°) 15 minutes, or until pastry is golden; cool completely on a rack.

3. Beat yolks slightly in a large saucepan, then stir in ½ cup of the sugar, salt and orange juice; sprinkle gelatin over top. Let stand several minutes to soften gelatin.
4. Cook slowly, stirring constantly, until mixture thickens and coats a spoon; remove from heat. Pour into a large bowl.
5. Place bowl in a pan of ice and water to speed setting. Chill, stirring several times, just until as thick as unbeaten egg white.
6. While gelatin mixture chills, add cream of tartar to egg whites in a large bowl; beat until foamy-white and double in volume. Beat in remaining ½ cup sugar, 1 tablespoon at a time, until meringue stands in firm peaks. Beat cream until stiff in a small bowl.
7. Fold meringue, then whipped cream into thickened gelatin mixture until no streaks of white remain. Spoon into cooled pastry shell. Chill several hours, or until firm.

DUXBURY MINCE PIE

Bake at 400° for 40 minutes.
Makes 1 nine-inch pie.

- 2 **cups cranberries, washed and stemmed**
- 1 **cup sugar**
- ¼ **cup water**
- 1 **can (1 pound, 6 ounces) mincemeat pie filling**
- 1 **package piecrust mix**

1. Combine cranberries with sugar and water in a medium-size saucepan. Heat, stirring constantly, to boiling; simmer, stirring often, 5 minutes; remove from heat. Stir in filling; cool.
2. Prepare piecrust mix, following label directions, or make pastry from your favorite double-crust recipe. Roll out half to a 12-inch round on a lightly floured pastry board; fit into a 9-inch pie plate; trim overhang to ½ inch. Spoon cranberry mixture into crust.
3. Roll out remaining pastry to a 10x8-inch rectangle; cut lengthwise into 10 strips. Weave strips over filling to make a crisscross top. Press edges together; turn under, flush with rim; flute to make a stand-up edge. Brush top lightly with milk and sprinkle with sugar, if you wish.
4. Bake in hot oven (400°) 40 minutes, or until juices bubble up and pastry is golden. Cool pie completely on a wire rack before serving.

SUGAR-FROSTED APPLE PIE

Bake at 425° for 35 minutes.
Makes 1 nine-inch pie.

- 2¼ cups sifted all-purpose flour
- ½ teaspoon salt
- 1 tablespoon grated lemon peel
- ¾ cup chilled vegetable shortening
- ¼ cup ice water
- 6 medium-size apples, pared, quartered, cored and sliced thin (2 pounds)
- 1 cup sugar
- 2½ tablespoons flour
- ¾ teaspoon ground cinnamon
- ¼ teaspoon ground nutmeg
- ¼ teaspoon ground mace
- ¼ teaspoon salt
- 2 tablespoons butter or margarine
- 1 tablespoon sugar (for topping)

1. Combine flour, salt and lemon rind in a medium-size bowl; cut in shortening with a pastry blender or 2 knives until mixture is crumbly. Sprinkle water over, a tablespoon at a time; mix quickly and lightly with a fork; gather dough together with fingers so it cleans the bowl; press into a ball; divide in half. Roll out half to a 12-inch round on a lightly floured pastry cloth or board; fit into a 9-inch pie plate. Trim overhang to ½ inch; reserve trimmings.
2. Mix sugar, 2½ tablespoons flour, cinnamon, nutmeg, mace and ¼ teaspoon salt in a large bowl; add apple slices; toss gently to mix; spoon into prepared pastry shell; dot with butter or margarine.
3. Roll out remaining pastry to an 11-inch round; cut an "x" slit near center to allow steam to escape; carefully place pastry evenly on top of filling; trim overhang to ½ inch; turn edges under and press together to seal; flute rim or make your favorite edging; fold back the 4 points of the center slit.
4. Brush top of pastry lightly with water; sprinkle with the 1 tablespoon of sugar.
5. Roll out pastry trimmings; with small hors d'oeuvre cutter or sharp knife, make leaf shapes; brush with water and extra sugar; place on baking sheet.
6. Bake pie in hot oven (425°) 35 minutes, or until apples are tender. Bake pastry leaves until golden, about 15 minutes.
7. To serve: Place pastry leaves around center slit. Cut leaf shapes from sliced Cheddar cheese; arrange around leaves, if you wish.

ROSE CHIFFON PIE

Bake shell at 350° for 10 minutes.
Makes 1 nine-inch pie.

- 2 cans (4½ ounces each) whole blanched almonds, ground (2 cups)
- 2 tablespoons butter or margarine, softened
- 3 tablespoons sugar (for crust)
- 1 envelope unflavored gelatin
- ¾ cup sugar (for filling)
- 4 eggs, separated
- ½ cup Rose wine
- ¼ cup water
- ¼ teaspoon cream of tartar
- 1 cup cream for whipping
- 5 drops red food coloring

1. Blend almonds, butter or margarine, and the 3 tablespoons sugar in a small bowl. Press evenly over bottom and side of a very lightly buttered 9-inch pie plate.
2. Bake in moderate oven (350°) 10 minutes, or until lightly golden. Cool completely on a wire rack.
3. Mix gelatin and ½ cup of the sugar in the top of a double boiler; beat in egg yolks until light and fluffy; blend in wine and water; place over simmering water. Cook, stirring constantly, until gelatin dissolves and mixture coats a spoon; pour into a large bowl.
4. Set bowl in a pan of ice water to speed setting. Chill at room temperature, stirring often, just until as thick as unbeaten egg white.
5. While gelatin mixture chills, beat egg whites with cream of tartar until foamy-white and double in volume in a medium-size bowl; beat in remaining ¼ cup sugar, 1 tablespoon at a time, beating all the time, until meringue stands in firm peaks. Beat cream until stiff in a second medium-size bowl.
6. Fold meringue, then whipped cream into thickened gelatin mixture until no streaks of white remain; fold in about 5 drops of food coloring to tint pink. Chill again, if necessary, until thick enough to mound when spooned. Spoon into cooled crust. Chill at least 4 hours, or until firm. Just before serving, garnish with whipped cream, if you wish.

FRUITED SOUR CREAM PIE

Bake at 400° for 40 minutes.
Makes 1 nine-inch pie.

½ **package piecrust mix**
3 **eggs**
1 **cup sugar**
¼ **teaspoon salt**
¼ **teaspoon ground cinnamon**
1½ **cups dairy sour cream**
1 **package (8 ounces) pitted dates, cut up**
½ **cup golden raisins**

1. Prepare piecrust mix, following label directions, or make pastry from your favorite single-crust recipe. Roll out to a 12-inch round on a lightly floured pastry board; fit into a 9-inch pie plate. Trim overhang to ½ inch; turn under, flush with rim; flute to make a standup edge.
2. Beat eggs until foamy in a medium-size bowl. Stir in sugar, salt, cinnamon and sour cream, until blended. Stir in dates and raisins. Pour into prepared pastry shell, spreading evenly.
3. Bake in hot oven (400°) 40 minutes, or until filling is puffy and set. Cool completely on a wire rack. Serve plain or with ice cream.

MINCEMEAT-PEAR PIE

Bake at 400° for 45 minutes.
Makes 1 nine-inch pie.

½ **package piecrust mix**
1 **large lemon**
3 **large fresh pears**
1 **jar (1 pound, 12 ounces) prepared mincemeat**
¾ **cup all-purpose flour**
¼ **cup sugar**
½ **teaspoon pumpkin-pie spice**
¼ **cup (½ stick) butter or margarine**

1. Prepare piecrust mix, following label directions, or make pastry from your favorite single-crust recipe. Roll out to a 12-inch round on a lightly floured pastry board; fit into a 9-inch pie plate. Trim overhang to ½ inch; turn under, flush with rim; flute to make a stand-up edge.
2. Grate 1 teaspoon lemon rind; reserve. Squeeze lemon; measure 2 tablespoons; reserve.
3. Pare pears; quarter and core. Slice 1 of the pears into wedges in a small bowl; sprinkle lemon juice over top, then toss lightly to coat well. Chop remaining pears finely.
4. Combine chopped pears, lemon rind, mincemeat and ¼ cup of the flour in a medium-size bowl. Spoon into prepared pastry shell. Arrange pear wedges on top, pinwheel fashion.
5. Combine remaining ½ cup flour, sugar and pumpkin-pie spice in a small bowl. Cut in butter or margarine with a pastry blender or two knives until crumbly. Sprinkle crumbs over pie.
6. Bake in hot oven (400°) 45 minutes, or until crumbs are golden-brown and filling is bubbly. Cool completely on a wire rack.
7. To match our picture (page 74), garnish with a lemon rose. Choose a medium-size lemon and, starting at the stem end pare off rind in one continuous long strip. Rewind spiral, following natural curl. Stand on stem end; curl spiral as tight as you wish to resemble rose.

COCONUT CUSTARD PIE

Bake at 425° for 3 minutes, then at 325° for 40 minutes.
Makes 1 nine-inch pie.

½ **package piecrust mix**
3 **cups milk**
4 **eggs**
⅓ **cup sugar**
¼ **teaspoon salt**
1 **can (3½ ounces) flaked coconut**
½ **teaspoon grated lemon rind**
1 **teaspoon vanilla**

1. Prepare piecrust mix, following label directions, or make your favorite one-crust recipe. Roll out to a 12-inch round on a lightly floured pastry board; fit into a 9-inch pie plate. Trim overhang to ½ inch; turn edge under, flush with rim; flute to make a stand-up edge.
2. Bake in hot oven (425°) 3 minutes; cool on a rack. Lower oven temperature to (325°).
3. Heat milk very slowly in a medium-size saucepan until bubbles appear around edge.
4. Beat eggs slightly in a large bowl; stir in sugar and salt; slowly stir in scalded milk. Strain into another bowl; stir in coconut, lemon rind and vanilla. Pour into partly baked pastry shell.
5. Bake in slow oven (325°) 40 minutes, or until center is almost set but still soft. (Do not overbake; custard will set as it cools.) Cool.

GLAZED APPLE JALOUSIE

Bake at 400° for 30 minutes.
Makes 6 servings.

- ¼ cup currants or raisins
- 2 teaspoons grated lemon rind
- ⅓ cup sugar
- ¼ teaspoon ground cardamom
- 2 tablespoons butter or margarine
- 1 package (10 ounces) frozen patty shells, thawed
- 1 can (1 pound, 4 ounces) unsweetened sliced apples, drained
- 1 egg, beaten
- ⅓ cup apple or crab apple jelly, melted

1. Heat oven to 450°.
2. Combine currants, lemon rind, sugar and cardamom. Blend in butter or margarine with a fork.
3. Overlap 3 patty shells on a lightly floured board; overlap remaining 3 patty shells next to them so that all are overlapped. Roll out to a 13x12-inch rectangle.
4. Place a double thickness of 12-inch aluminum foil on a cooky sheet. Cut a 13x5-inch piece of pastry; place on foil. Cover center of pastry with ⅓ of the apples; sprinkle with ⅓ of the sugar mixture. Add more apples and sugar mixture; repeat same procedure for top layer of the pastry.
5. From remaining pastry cut 4 pastry strips ½ inch wide and 13 inches long; cut each in half. Brush edges of pastry base with beaten egg. Place strips in 4 crisscross patterns over apples, pressing ends onto base.
6. Cut remaining pastry into 1-inch strips. Place the strips along all 4 edges of pastry base to fasten down the crisscrosses and seal in filling. Press firmly into place. Brush all surfaces with beaten egg.
7. Carefully fold edges of foil to contain pastry. This will help keep the shape of the pastry as it bakes in the oven.
8. Place in very hot oven (450°). Immediately lower heat to 400°. Bake 30 minutes, or until pastry is golden. Cool a few minutes on cooky sheet.
9. Carefully remove from foil and cooky sheet to wire rack. While still hot, brush jalousie with melted jelly, coating both pastry and filling. Serve slightly warm.

SWEET-POTATO PIE

Bake at 425° for 5 minutes, then at 425° for 40 minutes.
Makes 1 nine-inch pie.

- Rich Pastry (recipe follows)
- 1 pound sweet potatoes
- 3 eggs
- ½ cup firmly packed dark brown sugar
- ½ teaspoon salt
- ½ teaspoon ground cinnamon
- ¼ teaspoon ground nutmeg
- ⅛ teaspoon ground ginger
- 1 tall can evaporated milk
- 1 cup heavy cream
- 1 tablespoon molasses

1. Make Rich Pastry. Roll out to a 12-inch round on a lightly floured pastry cloth or board; fit into a 9-inch pie plate. Trim overhang to ½ inch; turn under, flush with rim; flute to make a stand-up edge. Chill while making the sweet-potato filling.
2. Pare sweet potatoes and dice. Cook, covered, in boiling slightly salted water in a medium-size saucepan 15 minutes or until tender.
3. Drain the potatoes; shake in pan over low heat to dry. Mash, then beat until smooth with an electric beater.
4. Beat eggs slightly in a large bowl; stir in brown sugar, salt, spices, sweet potatoes and milk. Pour the egg-potato-milk mixture into chilled pastry shell.
5. Bake in hot oven (425°) 5 minutes; lower oven temperature to slow (325°). Bake 40 minutes, or until center is almost set but still soft. (Do not overbake, for custard will set as it cools.) Cool pie on a wire rack until you're ready to serve dessert.
6. When ready to serve, mix cream and molasses in a medium-size bowl; beat until stiff. Spoon onto pie.

RICH PASTRY: Combine 1½ cups sifted all-purpose flour and ½ teaspoon salt in a large bowl; cut in ¼ cup shortening and 4 tablespoons (½ stick) butter or margarine with a pastry blender until mixture is crumbly. Sprinkle with 4 tablespoons cold water, 1 tablespoon at a time; mix lightly with a fork just until pastry holds together and leaves side of bowl clean.

Frozen Specialties/6

As long as ice cream, whipped cream and chocolate sauce are
around, soda parlor desserts will never go out of style.
Except today you no longer have to budge from home to enjoy
the most captivating ice cream creation. In this chapter
we show you how easy it is, by adding a few extra ingredients
to store-bought ice cream. And for nostalgia buffs, we've
included recipes for making your own ice cream,
as well as other delightful frozen specialties.
So pull up a soda chair, and read on!

Fresh fruit sherbets in six flavors (from left to right, top): Lime, Strawberry and Lemon; (bottom), Pineapple Coconut, Orange and Apricot. The recipes for these desserts are in this chapter.

HOW TO UNMOLD SHERBET

Run a thin-bladed knife around edge of mold or bowl. Invert mold onto a chilled serving plate. Moisten a clean cloth under hot running water; wring out as well as possible; press cloth against side of mold. Continue with hot cloths until sherbet melts just enough for mold to loosen; lift off mold. Return sherbet to freezer until serving time.

STRAWBERRY SHERBET

Makes 1½ quarts.

2 pints fresh strawberries (4 cups)
2 cups sugar
3 containers (8 ounces each) plain yogurt

1. Wash, hull and slice strawberries. Beat strawberries and sugar in large bowl of electric mixer at medium speed 2 minutes, or until strawberries are crushed and sugar is dissolved; blend in yogurt.
2. Pour strawberry-yogurt mixture into 9-inch square pan; freeze until firm, about 3 hours.
3. Break frozen mixture into chunks in a chilled large bowl. Beat with electric mixer until smooth, about 5 minutes.
4. Spoon sherbet into chilled 6-cup mold or bowl. Cover with foil or plastic wrap; freeze about 6 hours, or overnight. Unmold, or scoop directly from bowl.

APRICOT SHERBET

Makes 6 cups.

2 cans (15 ounces each) apricot halves, drained
¾ cup apricot nectar
½ cup sugar
2 tablespoons lemon juice
1 teaspoon chopped preserved ginger
2 egg whites

1. Combine apricot halves, nectar, ⅓ cup of the sugar, lemon juice and ginger in container of electric blender. Whirl until mixture is smooth and sugar is completely dissolved, about 1½ minutes. Pour into a 9-inch square pan. Place in freezer until frozen 2 inches in from edge, about 2 hours.
2. Beat egg whites until foamy-white. Beat in remaining sugar slowly, until meringue forms soft peaks.
3. Spoon apricot mixture into a chilled large bowl. Beat with electric mixer until mixture is smooth.
4. Fold meringue into apricot mixture. Spoon into a 6-cup mold or bowl. Cover with foil or plastic wrap; freeze 6 hours, or overnight. Unmold or scoop directly from bowl.

ROMAN HOLIDAY SHERBET

Makes 1½ quarts.

2 oranges
2 lemons
2 limes
1¼ cups sugar
1 envelope unflavored gelatin
1 cup water
2 cups dry white wine
2 egg whites
¼ cup sugar

1. Grate rind from oranges, lemons and limes. Squeeze fruits and strain juices into a 2-cup measure, adding water, if necessary, to make 1½ cups.
2. Combine the 1¼ cups sugar and gelatin in a medium-size saucepan; stir in water and rinds.
3. Heat, stirring often, until mixture comes to boiling; lower heat and simmer 5 minutes. Remove saucepan from heat; stir in fruit juices. Strain mixture into a 13x9x2-inch metal pan.
4. Cool at room temperature 30 minutes. Stir in wine until well-blended. Freeze mixture, stirring several times so that sherbet freezes evenly, until almost frozen, about 4 hours.
5. Beat egg whites until foamy and double in volume in a small bowl. Beat in the ¼ cup sugar, a tablespoon at a time, until meringue forms soft glossy peaks.
6. Spoon frozen mixture into a chilled large bowl. Beat with an electric mixer until mixture is very smooth.
7. Fold in meringue quickly. Spoon into a 6-cup mold or bowl; cover with foil or plastic wrap.
8. Freeze about 6 hours, or overnight. Unmold, or scoop directly from bowl.

Opposite page: Strawberry Meringue Cake (center). Recipe is in this chapter. Below: Elegant Strawberry Mousse (left) and Strawberry Charlotte. Recipes are in Chapter 8.

LEMON SHERBET

Makes 1½ quarts.

1¼ cups sugar
1 envelope unflavored gelatin
2¼ cups water
1 tablespoon grated lemon rind
½ cup lemon juice
1½ cups milk
2 egg whites
¼ cup sugar

1. Combine the 1¼ cups sugar and unflavored gelatin in a medium-size saucepan; stir in water and lemon rind.
2. Heat, stirring often, until mixture comes to boiling; lower heat and simmer 5 minutes; remove saucepan from heat; stir in lemon juice. Strain mixture into a 13x9x2-inch metal pan.
3. Cool at room temperature 30 minutes. Stir in milk until well-blended. Freeze mixture, stirring several times so that sherbet freezes evenly, until almost frozen, about 4 hours.
4. Beat egg whites until foamy and double in volume in a small bowl. Beat in the ¼ cup sugar, a tablespoon at a time, until meringue forms soft peaks.
5. Spoon frozen mixture into a chilled large bowl. Beat with an electric mixer until mixture is very smooth.
6. Fold in meringue, quickly. Spoon into a 6-cup mold or bowl; cover with foil or plastic wrap.
7. Freeze at least 6 hours, or overnight. Unmold, or scoop right from bowl.

PINEAPPLE COCONUT SHERBET

Makes 1½ quarts.

1 small ripe pineapple
½ cup sugar
1 envelope unflavored gelatin
¼ cup water
1½ cups (1-pound can) cream of coconut or coconut milk cream
2 egg whites
3 tablespoons sugar
1 tablespoon rum

1. Pare, halve and core pineapple. Chop very fine, or put through a food grinder, using fine blade. Measure out 2 cups of the pineapple.
2. Combine pineapple and the ½ cup sugar in a large bowl; mix well; let stand ½ hour.
3. Soften gelatin in water in a small saucepan. Place over very low heat until gelatin dissolves and mixture is clear.
4. Stir gelatin into pineapple-sugar mixture; blend in cream of coconut; pour mixture into a 9-inch square pan; freeze until mixture is firm (about 3 hours).
5. Break frozen mixture into chunks in a chilled large bowl. Beat with electric mixer until mixture is smooth, about 5 minutes.
6. Beat egg whites until foamy-white. Beat in remaining sugar, a tablespoon at a time, until meringue forms soft peaks. Fold meringue into pineapple-coconut mixture; stir in rum.
7. Spoon sherbet into chilled 6-cup mold or bowl. Cover with foil or plastic wrap; freeze about 6 hours, or overnight. Unmold, or scoop directly from bowl.

LIME SHERBET

Makes 1½ quarts.

1¼ cups sugar
1 envelope unflavored gelatin
2¼ cups water
1 tablespoon grated lime rind
½ cup lime juice
1½ cups milk
2 egg whites
¼ cup sugar
Few drops green food coloring

1. Combine the 1¼ cups sugar and gelatin in a medium-size saucepan; stir in water and lime rind.
2. Heat, stirring often, until mixture comes to boiling; lower heat and simmer 5 minutes. Remove saucepan from heat; stir in lime juice. Strain mixture into a 13x9x2-inch metal pan.
3. Cool at room temperature 30 minutes. Stir in milk until well-blended. Freeze mixture, stirring several times so that sherbet freezes evenly, until almost frozen, about 4 hours.
4. Beat egg whites until foamy and double in volume in a small bowl. Beat in the ¼ cup sugar, a tablespoon at a time, until meringue forms soft peaks.
5. Spoon frozen mixture into a chilled large

bowl. Beat with an electric mixer until mixture is very smooth.

6. Fold in meringue quickly. Tint mixture a pale green with a few drops green food coloring. Spoon into a 6-cup mold or bowl; cover with foil or plastic wrap.

7. Freeze at least 6 hours, or overnight. Unmold, or scoop directly from bowl.

BRANDIED PEACH ICE CREAM

Makes about 2 quarts.

    4 medium-size peaches, peeled, pitted and
      diced (about 2 cups)
    ¼ cup brandy
    3 cups heavy cream
    1 cup sugar

1. Toss peaches with brandy in a large bowl; mash slightly.

2. Combine 1 cup of the cream with sugar in a small saucepan; heat slowly, stirring constantly, until sugar dissolves. Pour over peach mixture; stir in remaining 2 cups cream.

3. Pour mixture into a 4-to-6-quart freezer can; freeze, following manufacturer's directions.

FRESH STRAWBERRY ICE CREAM

Makes about 2 quarts.

 1¼ cups sugar
     Dash of salt
    3 tablespoons flour
 1½ cups milk
    3 eggs, slightly beaten
    3 cups heavy cream
    1 pint strawberries, washed and hulled
      Few drops red food coloring

1. Combine 1 cup of the sugar, salt and flour in a medium-size saucepan; add milk gradually. Cook over medium heat, stirring, until mixture thickens and bubbles. Remove from heat.

2. Stir half the mixture slowly into beaten eggs in a medium-size bowl; stir back into remaining mixture in saucepan. Cook, stirring constantly, 1 minute. Remove from heat; pour into a large bowl; cool; stir in cream. Chill.

3. Mash strawberries with a potato masher or

a fork in a large bowl; stir in remaining ¼ cup sugar. Blend strawberries into chilled mixture; add food coloring for a deeper pink, if you wish.

4. Pour mixture into a 4-to-6-quart freezer can; freeze, following manufacturer's directions.

BROWNIE CREAM CAKE

Bake at 350° for 25 minutes.
Makes 8 to 10 servings.

    1 package (about 1 pound) brownie mix
      Eggs
      Water
    1 pint pistachio ice cream
    1 pint vanilla ice cream
 1½ cups heavy cream
    ¼ cup sugar

1. Grease 2 eight-inch layer-cake pans; line bottoms with wax paper; grease the paper, then dust lightly with flour.

2. Prepare brownie mix with eggs and water, following label directions for cakelike brownies; pour evenly into prepared pans.

3. Bake in moderate oven (350°) 25 minutes, or until firm. Cool in pans on wire racks 10 minutes; turn out onto racks; peel off paper. Cool layers completely.

4. Wash one of the cake pans; dry well. Line smoothly with foil, allowing a 2-inch overhang.

5. Spoon about one third of the pistachio ice cream into pan to make a ring around edge, then make an inner ring with part of the vanilla ice cream and fill center with pistachio. Top with a second layer of rings, alternating colors. (Job goes quickly if you use a teaspoon and scoop up the ice cream in small petal shapes.) Cover pan; freeze several hours, or until firm.

6. When ready to put dessert together, beat cream with sugar until stiff in a medium-size bowl.

7. Unmold ice cream by pulling up on foil; peel off foil, then stack ice-cream layer between brownie layers on a cooky sheet. Frost cake all over with part of the whipped cream.

8. Attach a fancy tip to a pastry bag; fill bag with remaining whipped cream; press out around side and top of cake. Freeze overnight.

9. About a half hour before serving, remove cake from freezer; place on a serving plate; let stand in refrigerator to soften for easy slicing.

LEMON VELVET ICE CREAM

Makes 3 quarts.

    2 cups sugar
    ¼ teaspoon salt
    3 tablespoons flour
 3 ½ cups milk
    6 egg yolks, slightly beaten
    2 tablespoons grated lemon rind
    ⅔ cup lemon juice
    3 cups heavy cream

1. Combine sugar, salt and flour in a large saucepan; add milk gradually. Cook over medium heat, stirring constantly, until mixture thickens and bubbles. Remove from heat.
2. Stir half the mixture slowly into beaten egg yolks; stir back into remaining mixture in saucepan. Cook, stirring constantly, 1 minute. Remove from heat; pour into a large bowl; cool. Add lemon rind and lemon juice. Stir in cream; chill.
3. Pour mixture into a 4-to-6-quart freezer can; freeze, following manufacturer's directions.
4. Pack in plastic containers; freeze until firm.

ORANGE SHERBET

Makes 1½ quarts.

 1 ¼ cups sugar
    1 envelope unflavored gelatin
 2 ¼ cups water
    1 tablespoon grated orange rind
    1 can (6 ounces) frozen concentrated orange juice
    1 cup milk
    2 egg whites
    ¼ cup sugar

1. Combine the 1¼ cups sugar and gelatin in a medium-size saucepan; stir in water and orange rind.
2. Heat, stirring often, until mixture comes to boiling; lower heat and simmer 5 minutes. Remove saucepan from heat; stir in frozen orange juice concentrate until thawed. Strain mixture into a 13x9x2-inch metal pan.
3. Cool at room temperature 30 minutes. Stir in milk until well-blended. Freeze mixture, stirring several times so that sherbet freezes evenly,

until almost frozen, approximately four hours.
4. Beat egg whites until foamy and double in volume in a small bowl. Beat in the ¼ cup sugar, a tablespoon at a time, until meringue forms soft peaks.
5. Spoon frozen mixture into a chilled large bowl. Beat immediately with an electric mixer until frozen mixture is very smooth.
6. Fold in meringue quickly. Spoon into a 6-cup mold or bowl; cover with foil or plastic wrap.
7. Freeze about 6 hours, or overnight. Unmold, or scoop directly from bowl.

RAINBOW ICE-CREAM CAKE

Bake at 350° for 30 minutes.
Makes 16 servings.

    1 package chocolate cake mix
    2 eggs
      Water
    1 quart strawberry ice cream, softened
    1 quart pistachio ice cream, softened
    2 envelopes (2 ounces each) whipped topping mix
      Milk
      Red food coloring
    1 tablespoon light rum (optional)
      Chopped pistachio nuts

1. Grease 2 nine-inch round layer-cake pans; dust with flour; tap out any excess.
2. Prepare cake mix with eggs and water, following label directions; pour into prepared pans.
3. Bake in moderate oven (350°) 30 minutes, or until centers spring back when lightly pressed with fingertip. Cool in pans on wire racks 10 minutes. Loosen layers around edges with a knife; turn out onto racks; cool completely. Split each layer, using a sawing motion with a sharp knife.
4. While layers bake, cut two 18-inch lengths of plastic wrap and fit into 2 eight-inch layer-cake pans.
5. Spread half the strawberry ice cream evenly in each cake pan. Top with half the pistachio ice cream in each pan. (Or use your favorite flavor combinations.) Cover ice cream with plastic wrap and freeze until ready to use.
6. Place one split cake layer on cooky sheet. Remove one ice cream layer from pan; peel

off transparent wrap and place on split layer; repeat with 2 more split layers and second ice-cream layer. (The extra split layer will make a nice treat for supper topped with a scoop of coffee ice cream.) Freeze entire cake while making frosting.

7. Beat whipped topping mix with milk, following label directions. Tint a pale pink with red food coloring and flavor with rum, if you wish.

8. Frost side and top of cake with part of frosting; pile remaining frosting onto center of cake and swirl out with teaspoon and sprinkle with pistachio nuts.

9. Freeze until frosting is firm; then cover with plastic wrap.

10. When ready to serve, loosen cake around edge of cooky sheet with a spatula dipped in hot water; transfer to serving plate with spatula and pancake turner. Cut with a sharp knife, or try your electric knife.

FROSTED ANGEL CROWN

Bake at 300° for 30 minutes.
Makes 6 to 8 servings.

   1 package yellow cake mix
   Whole eggs
   Water
   4 egg whites
   ¼ teaspoon cream of tartar
   ¾ cup sugar
   1 teaspoon vanilla
   2 pints peach ice cream
   2 packages (12 ounces each) frozen sliced peaches, thawed and drained

1. Prepare cake mix with whole eggs and water, bake in 2 nine-inch layer-cake pans, cool and remove from pans, following label directions. Wrap one layer and set aside for another day.

2. Beat egg whites and cream of tartar until foamy-white and double in volume in a large bowl; beat in sugar, 1 tablespoon at a time, until sugar dissolves completely and meringue stands in firm peaks; beat in vanilla.

3. Place cake layer on a cooky sheet; frost side and top with part of the meringue, then spread remaining around edge, building up edge to form a rim about an inch higher than cake layer.

4. Bake in slow oven (300°) 30 minutes, or until

meringue is lightly golden; cool on cooky sheet.

5. When ready to serve, loosen cake from cooky sheet with a spatula; place on a serving plate.

6. Fill center with spoonfuls of ice cream; garnish with peach slices. Cut in wedges.

WALNUT CRUNCH ICE CREAM

Makes 1 quart.

   ¼ cup (½ stick) butter or margarine
   6 tablespoons sugar
   ½ teaspoon light corn syrup
   1 tablespoon water
   Dash of salt
   ¼ cup chopped walnuts
   All-American Vanilla Ice Cream (page 92)

1. Combine butter or margarine, sugar, corn syrup, water and salt in a small heavy saucepan. Cook over medium heat, stirring constantly, until a candy thermometer reaches 305°. Add nuts; mix well.

2. Pour onto a buttered cooky sheet. Cool.

3. When candy is hardened, chop into small pieces.

4. Stir candy pieces into freshly made All-American Vanilla Ice Cream.

PHILADELPHIA ICE CREAM

Makes 1 quart.

   1 quart heavy cream
   ¾ cup sugar
   ¼ teaspoon salt
   1 two-inch piece vanilla bean
   OR: 2 tablespoons vanilla

1. Combine 2 cups of the cream, sugar and salt in a medium-size saucepan.

2. If using vanilla bean, cut in half, lengthwise, and scrape out the tiny seeds. Add seeds and pod to cream mixture in saucepan.

3. Heat, stirring often, just until sugar dissolves. Pour into a bowl and add remaining 2 cups cream and vanilla, if not using vanilla bean. Chill at least 1 hour.

4. If vanilla bean is used, remove pod before pouring into a 4-to-6-quart freezer can; freeze, following manufacturer's directions.

ALL-AMERICAN VANILLA ICE CREAM

Makes about 2 quarts.

1½ cups sugar
¼ cup flour
Dash of salt
2 cups milk
4 eggs, slightly beaten
1 quart heavy cream
2 tablespoons vanilla

1. Combine sugar, flour and salt in a large saucepan; stir in milk. Cook, stirring constantly, over medium heat, until mixture thickens and bubbles 1 minute.
2. Stir half the hot mixture slowly into beaten eggs in a medium-size bowl; stir back into remaining mixture in saucepan. Cook, stirring, 1 minute.
3. Pour into a large bowl; stir in cream and vanilla. Chill at least 2 hours.
4. Pour mixture into a 4-to-6-quart freezer can; freeze, following manufacturer's directions.

PEACH MELBA RIPPLE ICE CREAM

Makes 2 quarts.

1 cup sugar
3 tablespoons flour
Dash of salt
1½ cups milk
3 eggs, slightly beaten
3 cups heavy cream
½ teaspoon almond extract
2 packages (10 ounces each) frozen peaches, thawed and drained
1 package (10 ounces) frozen raspberries, thawed
2 tablespoons sugar
1 teaspoon cornstarch

1. Combine 1 cup sugar, flour and salt in a medium-size saucepan; add milk gradually. Cook over medium heat, stirring, until mixture thickens and bubbles. Remove from heat.
2. Stir half the mixture slowly into beaten eggs in a medium-size bowl; stir back into remaining mixture in saucepan. Cook, stirring constantly, 1 minute. Remove from heat; pour into bowl; cool. Stir in cream and extract and chill.

3. Crush peaches with potato masher or fork in a medium-size bowl; reserve.
4. Press raspberries through a fine sieve into a small saucepan; add 2 tablespoons sugar. Mix cornstarch and 1 tablespoon water in a cup; add to raspberries. Cook over medium heat, just until thickened and bubbly. Cool; reserve.
5. Pour ice cream mixture into a 4-to-6-quart freezer can; add peaches; freeze, following manufacturer's directions.
6. When ice cream is frozen, working very fast, spoon about one-fifth of the ice cream into a large plastic container or bowl; drizzle raspberry sauce over. Continue to layer the ice cream and sauce this way. Freeze until firm.
NOTE: If you wish to use fresh peaches in your ice cream, peel and crush 3 large peaches with ½ cup sugar. Continue as above.

APRICOT ICE CREAM

Makes about 2 quarts.

1 package (8 ounces) dried apricots
1½ cups water
1¾ cups sugar
¼ cup flour
Dash of salt
1½ cups milk
4 eggs, slightly beaten
1 quart heavy cream
1 tablespoon vanilla

1. Cover apricots with water in a small saucepan. Heat to boiling. Cover saucepan and remove from heat. Allow to stand 1 hour, or until almost all of the water has been absorbed. Pour apricots and liquid into container of electric blender; whirl until pureed, or press through sieve or food mill.
2. Combine sugar, flour and salt in a large saucepan; stir in milk. Cook, stirring constantly, over medium heat, until mixture thickens and bubbles 1 minute. Remove from heat.
3. Stir half of the mixture slowly into beaten eggs in a medium-size bowl; stir back into remaining mixture in saucepan. Cook, stirring constantly, 1 minute.
4. Pour into a large bowl; cool; stir in apricot puree, cream and vanilla. Chill.
5. Pour mixture into a 4-to-6-quart freezer can; freeze, following the manufacturer's directions.

MINT CHOCOLATE CHIP ICE CREAM

Makes 2 quarts.

1½ cups sugar
¼ cup flour
Dash of salt
2 cups milk
4 eggs, slightly beaten
1 quart heavy cream
¾ teaspoon green food coloring
2 teaspoons peppermint extract
1 square semisweet chocolate, finely chopped

1. Combine sugar, flour and salt in a medium-size saucepan; add milk gradually. Cook over medium heat, stirring constantly, until mixture thickens and bubbles. Remove from heat.
2. Stir one half the mixture slowly into beaten eggs in a medium-size bowl; stir back into remaining mixture in saucepan. Cook, stirring, 1 minute. Remove from heat; pour into bowl; cool. Stir in cream, coloring, extract; chill.
3. Pour into a 4-to-6-quart freezer can; freeze, following manufacturer's directions.
4. Fold chocolate into soft ice cream.

RASPBERRY SHERBET

Makes 2 quarts.

2 packages (10 ounces each) frozen red raspberries, thawed
1¾ cups sugar
Dash of salt
5 cups water
¼ cup lemon juice
2 egg whites
1 tall can evaporated milk, chilled
Few drops red food coloring

1. Press thawed raspberries and their syrup through a sieve to remove seeds; reserve.
2. Combine sugar, salt and water in a saucepan. Heat, stirring, just until sugar dissolves.
3. Remove from heat; stir in reserved puree and lemon juice; cool to warm.
4. Beat egg whites and evaporated milk until well blended in a large bowl; add raspberry mixture and stir well. Tint a brighter raspberry color with a few drops red food coloring.
5. Pour sherbet into a 4-to-6-quart freezer can; freeze, following the manufacturer's directions.

KONA CHOCOLATE ICE CREAM

Makes 2 quarts.

1½ cups sugar
¼ cup flour
2 teaspoons instant coffee powder
Dash of salt
2 cups milk
4 squares unsweetened chocolate
4 eggs, slightly beaten
1 quart heavy cream
2 tablespoons vanilla

1. Combine sugar, flour, coffee and salt in a large saucepan; stir in milk and chocolate.
2. Cook, stirring constantly, over medium heat, until chocolate melts and mixture thickens.
3. Stir half the mixture slowly into beaten eggs in a medium-size bowl; stir back into remaining mixture in saucepan. Cook, stirring, for about 1 minute.
4. Pour into a large bowl; stir in cream and vanilla. Chill.
5. Pour mixture into a 4-to-6-quart freezer can; freeze, following manufacturer's directions.

CHOCOLATE ICE CREAM SUPREME

Makes about 2 quarts.

1 cup milk
¼ cup dry cocoa (not a mix)
3 cups heavy cream
¼ cup finely chopped sweet cooking chocolate
6 egg yolks
1 cup sugar

1. Gradually add milk to cocoa in a medium-size saucepan, mixing until well-blended; add cream; heat slowly just until bubbles appear around edge. Stir in chocolate until melted.
2. Beat egg yolks until frothy in small bowl of mixer; gradually add sugar, beating until fluffy-thick. Stir a small portion of hot mixture into egg yolks; add to hot mixture in saucepan. Cook, stirring constantly, over low heat until mixture thickens slightly and coats a spoon. Strain into a bowl and chill until ready to freeze.
3. Pour mixture into a 4-to-6-quart freezer can; freeze, following the manufacturer's directions.

CHERRIES JUBILEE

Makes 6 to 8 servings.

 1 can (1 pound, 14 ounces) pitted black
   cherries
 3 tablespoons sugar
 2 tablespoons cornstarch
   Rind of 1 orange, grated
 ½ cup orange flavor liqueur, heated
   Vanilla ice cream

1. Drain cherry liquid into a 2 cup measure and
add water to make 1½ cups; reserve cherries.
2. Combine sugar and cornstarch in chafing pan
or medium-size skillet; stir in cherry liquid until very smooth; add orange rind.
3. Cook, stirring constantly, until mixture thickens and bubbles 1 minute. Add reserved cherries and heat until very warm.
4. Pour warmed orange liqueur over cherries
and ignite. Stir cherries until flame begins to die
down, then ladle over ice cream in individual
serving dishes.

STRAWBERRY MERINGUE CAKE

Bake at 350° for 30 minutes, then at 250° for
45 minutes.
Makes 12 servings.

Cake Layer:
 ⅔ cup sifted cake flour
 ¾ teaspoon baking powder
 ¼ teaspoon salt
 3 eggs
 ½ cup sugar
 1 teaspoon vanilla
Meringue:
 4 egg whites
   Dash of salt
 1 cup superfine granulated sugar
Filling:
 2 pints pistachio ice cream
   Strawberry Sauce Royale (recipe follows)

1. Make cake layer: Butter a 9x1½-inch layer-
cake pan; line pan with wax paper; cut to fit;
butter paper.
2. Measure flour, baking powder and salt into
sifter.
3. Beat eggs until foamy in a medium-size bowl;
gradually beat in sugar until mixture is very

thick and light (this is very important). Stir in
vanilla.
4. Sift dry ingredients over egg mixture; gently
fold in until no streaks of flour remain. Spread
batter evenly in prepared pan.
5. Bake in moderate oven (350°) 30 minutes,
or until center springs back when lightly pressed
with fingertip.
6. Cool cake in pan on a wire rack for 10 minutes; loosen cake around edge of pan and turn
upside down on wire rack; cool completely.
7. Make meringue: Beat egg whites with salt
in a medium-size bowl until foamy-white and
double in volume; add sugar, 1 tablespoon at a
time, beating until meringue stands in firm
peaks.
8. Line a cooky sheet with brown paper and
place cake layer on paper. Frost the top of
cake with a thin layer of meringue, then frost
the side thickly, swirling meringue with tip of
spatula. Fit a star tip into a pastry bag. Fill bag
with remaining meringue. Pipe a fancy border
around the tip of the cake, building up edge
about 1 inch.
9. Bake in very slow oven (250°) 45 minutes.
Turn off oven and allow meringue to cool in
oven at least 1 hour.
10. Loosen cake from brown paper with a long
spatula and slide onto serving plate. Scoop ice
cream balls into center of cake and spoon part
of Strawberry Sauce Royale over ice cream.
NOTE: Cake may be made the day before. Cake
can be filled several hours before serving and
frozen. Spoon sauce over, just before serving.

STRAWBERRY SAUCE ROYALE

Makes about 2½ cups.

 2 pints strawberries
 3 tablespoons cherry-flavored brandy
 ½ cup superfine granulated sugar

1. Wash and hull strawberries; dry well on paper toweling. Cut into thin slices.
2. Combine half of the berries and the cherry
brandy in the container of an electric blender;
cover. Whirl at high speed until smooth. (Or
mash half of the berries and add cherry brandy.)
3. Pour strawberry puree over sliced berries in
a medium-size bowl and add sugar. Chill several
hours before serving with the meringue cake.

Fast & Fabulous/7

Last-course favorites can be last-minute ones! This chapter proves the point by offering a first-class selection of desserts you can make in record time, without a passel of complicated steps. Some are classics updated and streamlined. Others are entirely new desserts that mix convenience with a large measure of imagination. All are guaranteed to make great eating an easy matter any day of the week, any hour of the day, any minute of the hour, any second of....

From left to right, top: Gâteau de Poires Helene, Easy Cheese Fruit Tarts and Black-Bottom Rum Pie. Middle: Peach Melba Bavarian, Coffee Parfait Pie and Mousse au Chocolat. Bottom: Quick Cherry Strudel and Choco-Raspberry Ice Box Cake. Recipes are in this chapter.

GATEAU DE POIRES HELENE

Preparation time: 12 minutes.
Makes 12 servings.

    1 eight to nine-inch baker's angel food cake
    1 can (1 pound) pear halves
    ¼ cup creme de cacao
    2 containers (6¾ ounces each) frozen
      whipped topping dessert, thawed
    1 can (5 ounces) vanilla pudding
    1 cup flaked coconut
      Fudge topping (from an 11-ounce jar)
      Toasted coconut (optional)

1. Split cake horizontally into 3 layers. Drain pears. Combine 2 tablespoons of the juice with creme de cacao, drizzle over cake layers.
2. Press about 1 cup of the whipped topping into a medium-size bowl; stir in vanilla pudding and flaked coconut. Then spread this filling on two of the cake layers.
3. Stack filled layers with plain layer on top, on serving plate. Arrange pear halves with narrow ends to the center on top layer.
4. Pipe remaining whipped topping onto side of cake and between pears on top. Just before serving, spoon fudge topping over the pears. To top off the cake, just sprinkle with toasted coconut, if you wish.
NOTE: To toast coconut, spread 2 tablespoons coconut onto small cooky sheet; place in slow oven (325°) about 8 to 10 minutes.

CHOCO-RASPBERRY ICE BOX CAKE

Preparation time: 15 minutes.
Chilling time: Several hours.
Makes 8 servings.

    ½ cup raspberry preserves
    2 tablespoons orange-flavored liqueur
    2 packages (two ounces each) whipped
      topping mix
    1 cup cold milk
    2 teaspoons vanilla
    1 package (8½ ounces) chocolate wafers

1. Combine raspberry preserves and orange flavor liqueur in a cup. Prepare topping mix with milk and vanilla, following label directions.
2. Spread raspberry mixture on one side of a chocolate wafer and whipped topping on sec-

ond side. Make 10 cooky stacks of coated cookies until all cookies are coated.
3. Turn the first cooky stack on its side on serving tray; spread last cooky with whipped topping and press on the next stack. Repeat until all cookies are joined in a long roll.
4. Frost cake generously with whipped topping. Fit a pastry bag with a fancy tip. Fill bag with remaining whipped topping. Pipe a double row of swirls down the center of cake. Pipe remaining whipped topping around sides and bottom of cake. Spoon remaining raspberry preserves down the top of cake.
5. Chill at least 3 hours. To serve: Cut cake into thin diagonal slices.

BLACK-BOTTOM RUM PIE

Preparation time: 20 minutes.
Chilling time: Several hours.
Makes one eight-inch pie.

    2 cans (5 ounces each) vanilla pudding cup
    2 cans (5 ounces each) chocolate pudding
      cup
    2 tablespoons rum
    1 envelope unflavored gelatin
    ¼ cup water
    1 eight or nine-inch prepared graham cracker
      pie shell
    1 container (9 ounces) non-dairy whipped
      topping
      Chocolate curls

1. Place vanilla pudding in a small bowl; combine chocolate pudding and rum in another small bowl, reserve.
2. Soften gelatin in the water in a 1-cup measure. Place over hot, not boiling, water in a small saucepan until gelatin dissolves.
3. Stir 2 tablespoons of the dissolved gelatin into the vanilla pudding; add remaining gelatin mixture to chocolate-rum mixture. Place bowl containing chocolate-rum mixture in a pan of ice and water to speed-set. Chill, stirring often, until as thick as unbeaten egg white; pour into prepared graham cracker pie shell.
4. Add 1 cup non-dairy whipped topping into vanilla pudding mixture; fold in carefully; pile on top of chocolate mixture; chill until firm.
5. To serve: Decorate with remaining non-dairy whipped topping and chocolate curls.

JUBILEE CREAM

Makes 4 servings.

> 1 package vanilla-flavor whipped-dessert mix
> 1 teaspoon almond extract
> ½ cup toasted slivered almonds
> 1 cup cherry pie filling (from a 1-pound, 5-ounce can)

1. Prepare dessert mix with milk and water, following label directions; stir in almond extract. Chill at least an hour.
2. In a small bowl, mix almonds into cherry pie filling. Fill each of 4 parfait glasses this way: Holding glass on its side, spoon about ¼ cup of the cherry mixture into glass, then spoon chilled dessert mixture carefully into the other half of glass.

PEACH MELBA BAVARIAN

Preparation time: 10 minutes.
Chilling time: Several hours.
Makes 8 servings.

> 1 package (3 ounces) lemon-flavored gelatin
> 1 envelope unflavored gelatin
> ¼ cup cold milk
> 1 cup boiling water
> 2 egg yolks
> ⅓ cup sugar
>   Dash of salt
> 2 tablespoons peach brandy
> 1 package (10 ounces) frozen peach slices, cut into small pieces
> 1 cup heavy cream
>   Bottled raspberry sundae topping

1. Combine lemon-flavored gelatin and unflavored gelatin in the container of an electric blender; pour cold milk over and allow to stand 1 minute.
2. Pour boiling water into container; cover; whirl at low speed 2 minutes; remove cover. Add egg yolks, sugar, salt and peach brandy.
3. Replace blender cover and remove feeder cap. Whirl at high speed, gradually adding pieces of frozen peaches until mixture is smooth. Add cream if you have room in container; whirl until well-blended. (If you don't have room, stir with a rubber scraper until cream is well-blended.)

4. Pour mixture into a 5-cup ring mold. Chill at least 2 hours before serving.
5. To serve: Run a thin-bladed knife around edges of mold. Dip mold quickly in and out of a pan of hot water. Invert onto serving plate. Spoon bottled raspberry topping over.

QUICK CHERRY STRUDEL

Preparation time: 30 minutes.
Baking time: 25 minutes.
Makes 1 large strudel.

> 1 package (10 ounces) frozen ready-to-bake puff pastry shells
> 1 can (1 pound, 5 ounces) prepared cherry pie filling
> 2 teaspoons grated lemon rind
> ¼ cup packaged bread crumbs
> 1 tablespoon milk
> ¼ cup sliced unblanched almonds
> 2 tablespoons sugar

1. Preheat oven to 450°.
2. Let pastry shells soften at room temperature for 20 minutes.
3. Combine cherry pie filling and lemon rind in a small bowl; reserve.
4. On a cloth-lined, well-floured board, overlap pastry shells in a straight line. Using a floured stockinette-covered rolling pin, press down onto the pastry shells. (Note: You may use a floured rolling pin without the stockinette, but flour the rolling pin frequently to prevent the pastry shells from sticking.) Roll out from center of pastry shells to a 16x22-inch rectangle, being careful not to tear pastry.
5. Sprinkle pastry with bread crumbs.
6. Spoon cherry pie filling down length of pastry closest to you into a 2-inch strip and within 2 inches of edges. Fold in sides.
7. Using the pastry cloth, grasp at both ends and gently lift the cloth up and let the strudel roll itself up. Carefully slide onto a cooky sheet, keeping seam side down, and form into a horseshoe shape.
8. Brush top generously with milk; sprinkle on almond slices, pressing well in order to keep in place. Then sprinkle with sugar.
9. Lower oven heat to hot (400°), 25 minutes or until golden brown; let cool on baking sheet 10 minutes. Serve the strudel while still warm.

MOUSSE AU CHOCOLAT

Preparation time: 10 minutes.
Chilling time: 1 hour.
Makes 8 servings.

   1 package (8 ounces) semisweet chocolate pieces
   ⅓ cup hot, brewed coffee
   4 egg yolks
   2 tablespoons apricot brandy, or any fruit-flavored brandy
   4 egg whites
   3 tablespoons sugar

1. Combine chocolate pieces and hot coffee in the container of an electric blender; cover container. Whirl at high speed for 30 seconds, or until smooth.
2. Add egg yolks and brandy to container; cover. Whirl at high speed 30 seconds.
3. Beat egg whites until foamy and double in volume in a medium-size bowl; gradually beat in sugar until well-blended. Fold in chocolate mixture until no streaks of white remain. Spoon the prepared mousse into 8 parfait glasses or a serving bowl.
4. Chill at least 1 hour. To serve: Garnish with whipped cream and party candy-patties (from an 11-ounce package).

EASY CHEESE FRUIT TARTS

Preparation time: 5 minutes.
Chilling time: 30 minutes.
Makes 6 servings.

   2 packages (3 ounces each) cream cheese
   ½ cup milk
   1 can (9¾ ounces) raspberry or pineapple dessert mix
   1 package (5 ounces) pastry tart shells (6 to a package)
   Fresh or canned fruits for garnish
   Chopped pistachio nuts or almonds

1. Beat cream cheese until soft in a small bowl. Gradually beat in milk; continue beating until completely smooth. Add dessert mix; stir with a spoon 30 seconds, or until thickened.
2. Spoon into tart shells, dividing evenly. Decorate with fruits of your choice; sprinkle with nuts, if you wish. Chill until ready to serve.

QUICK SPICY RICE PUDDING

Makes 6 servings.

   1 cup packaged precooked rice
   2¾ cups milk
   1 package (about 3½ ounces) vanilla pudding and pie filling mix
   2 tablespoons raisins
   ⅛ teaspoon ground nutmeg
   1 tablespoon cinnamon-sugar

1. Combine rice and 2 cups of the milk in a medium-size saucepan; heat to boiling, stirring constantly; reduce heat; cover. Cook over low heat 5 minutes.
2. Add pudding mix to remaining milk; mix well. Stir into rice mixture. Bring to boiling, stirring constantly; stir in raisins and nutmeg. Turn into serving dish. Sprinkle with cinnamon-sugar. Chill 15 minutes, or until serving time.

RASPBERRY SNOW WITH CUSTARD SAUCE

Makes 6 servings.

   1 package (3 ounces) raspberry-flavor gelatin
   ¾ cup boiling water
   10 ice cubes
   2 egg whites
   Custard Sauce (recipe follows)

1. Dissolve gelatin in boiling water in container of electric blender; add ice cubes; blend at low speed until ice melts and gelatin starts to thicken. Add egg whites. (Save yolks for Custard Sauce.)
2. Blend at high speed until mixture triples in volume and starts to hold its shape.
3. Spoon into a 5-cup mold. Chill 1 hour, or until firm.
4. Just before serving, loosen around edge with a knife; dip mold very quickly in and out of a bowl of hot water. Cover with a plate; turn upside down; lift off mold. Serve with sauce.

CUSTARD SAUCE: Beat egg yolks with 2 tablespoons sugar and 1 teaspoon cornstarch in top of a double boiler; beat in 1 cup milk. Cook, stirring constantly, over hot, not boiling water 10 minutes, or until custard thickens slightly. Remove from heat; strain into a bowl; stir in 1 teaspoon vanilla. Cover; chill. Makes 1¼ cups.

COFFEE PARFAIT PIE

Preparation time: 10 minutes.
Chilling time: 1 hour.
Makes 8 to 10 servings.

  3 pints coffee ice cream
  3 envelopes unflavored gelatin
⅓ cup golden rum
  1 tablespoon instant coffee
⅔ cup water
  1 eight- or nine-inch prepared graham
     cracker pie shell
     Chocolate syrup
     Pecan halves

1. Remove ice cream from freezer to room temperature.
2. Sprinkle gelatin into rum in a 1-cup measure to soften, 5 minutes.
3. Combine instant coffee and water in a small saucepan, bring to boiling. Add softened gelatin; stir until completely dissolved.
4. Turn ice cream into a large bowl. Beat with electric mixer at high speed, until smooth. Pour gelatin in, all at once, while beating constantly and guiding mixture into beater with rubber spatula. (Mixture sets softly almost at once.)
5. Spoon into pie shell, mounding high in center, or pipe through a pastry bag fitted with a decorative tip. Chill until ready to serve. Just before serving, drizzle chocolate syrup over top and garnish with pecans, if you wish.

VIENNESE FRUIT TART

Makes 8 servings.

  1 can (6 ounces) frozen orange juice
     concentrate
  1 nine-and-a-half inch packaged sponge
     layer (6 ounces)
     OR: 1 nine-inch baked pastry shell
  1 package (3 ounces) cream cheese
  2 cans (5 ounces each) vanilla pudding
  1 banana
  1 can (1 pound) apricot halves
½ pint fresh raspberries
     OR: 1 package (10 ounces) frozen red
     raspberries, thawed and drained
½ pound (1 cup) seedless green grapes
½ cup apple jelly

1. Heat orange juice concentrate in a small saucepan just until hot.
2. Place cake on serving dish; brush generously with orange juice.
3. Stir cream cheese until very soft in a small bowl; stir in pudding. Spread mixture into bottom of cake layer.
4. Cut banana lengthwise into quarters; halve each quarter. Arrange 5 pieces of banana on pudding layer to form section dividers. Arrange apricot halves, raspberries and green grapes in a pattern in each section.
5. Heat apple jelly in a small saucepan until melted; brush over all fruits. Chill.

DIVIDENDS FOR DESSERTS

Tutti-frutti parfait: Drain a 1-pound can of fruit cocktail; combine fruit with a 6-ounce can of frozen concentrate for pineapple juice. Layer into parfait glasses with vanilla ice cream. Top each with a maraschino cherry.

Peanut cream: Blend ¼ cup cream-style or crunchy peanut butter with ¼ cup milk; stir in ½ cup prepared marshmallow cream. Spoon over plain custard.

Vermont cream mold: Line a 6-cup mold or bowl with waxed paper. Then fill with alternating layers of ladyfingers and butter-pecan ice cream, drizzling each layer with maple-flavor pancake syrup. Cover and freeze at least 4 hours. Serve with whipped cream and pecans.

Double butterscotch: Fix butterscotch pudding with a mix, following label directions; cool slightly. Fold in some butterscotch-flavor pieces. They'll give pudding a delightful crunch.

Sandwich stacks: Spread large thin chocolate wafers with chocolate-chip mint ice cream; stack three high; freeze.

Prune-whip topper: Beat 1 cup cream until stiff; fold in a 4-ounce jar of baby-pack strained prunes and 1 teaspoon grated orange rind. Spoon over squares of plain cake.

Jiffy Melba: Top plain vanilla pudding (made from a mix) with sliced fresh peaches and a dollop of red-raspberry preserves.

Big Moment Desserts / 8

Big moments demand celebration. And whether it's a birthday, holiday or the first day of spring, there's no better way to toast the day than with a beautiful dinner followed by an equally appealing dessert such as the Peach Bavarian shown on our cover. Or, perhaps you'd prefer something high, light and chocolaty like Cherry Cordial Chocolate Soufflé. This chapter includes both dramatic offerings plus a host of others you'll find delightful and delicious. First, there's a section of recipes for non-filling fruit desserts, the perfect follow-up to a big dinner. Then there are Bavarians, mousses and gelatins; the best cheesecakes ever to grace your table, eclairs, cream puffs and one section devoted to extra, extra specials. All are designed to make every day a very big moment.

Clockwise, from top: Chestnut Bavarian Cream, Queen of Puddings, Rice Imperatrice with Cherry Sauce, Wine Jelly With Fruits and Steamed Date-Walnut Pudding with Hard Sauce Pinwheels. Recipes for Queen of Puddings, Wine Jelly and Date-Walnut Pudding are in Chapter 4; others are in this chapter.

FRUIT DESSERTS

MERINGUE APPLES

Bake at 350° for 30 minutes; then for 6 minutes.
Makes 6 servings.

- **1 package (3¼ ounces) vanilla pudding and pie filling**
- **3 egg yolks**
- **2 cups milk**
- **1 cup light cream**
- **1 teaspoon rum extract**
- **3 large apples (about 2 pounds)**
- **½ cup finely chopped walnuts**
- **¼ cup honey**
- **½ teaspoon ground cinnamon**
- **3 tablespoons butter or margarine**
- **6 ladyfingers or pound cake slices**
- **3 egg whites**
- **¼ teaspoon cream of tartar**
- **⅓ cup sugar**
  Golden "Spun" Sugar (recipe follows)

1. Combine pudding mix, egg yolks, milk and cream in large saucepan; bring just to boiling, stirring constantly. Pour into a bowl. Stir in rum extract. Place a sheet of wax paper directly on surface of custard; chill.
2. Pare and core apples, then cut each in half crosswise. Place apples, cut side down, in 13x-9x2-inch baking pan.
3. Combine nuts, honey and cinnamon in a small bowl; fill into centers of apples, dividing evenly. Dot with butter or margarine.
4. Bake in moderate oven (350°) 30 minutes, brushing apples occasionally with pan juices. Cool slightly; keep brushing with juices. Place each apple on a split ladyfinger on cooky sheet.
5. Beat egg whites with cream of tartar until foamy and double in volume in a medium-size bowl. Gradually beat in sugar until meringue stands in firm peaks when beater is lifted. Spread meringue over apples, dividing evenly, or pipe through a pastry bag.
6. Bake at 350° for 6 minutes, or until lightly browned.
7. About an hour before serving, pour custard into a large shallow glass bowl. Gently set apples into custard. Drizzle with Golden "Spun" Sugar, waving spoon from apple to apple to "spin" sugar in threads. Chill before serving.

Going clockwise from top left are: Cathedral Cake, Frozen Neapolitan Dessert and Viennese Fruit Tart. Recipe for Tart is in Chapter 7; others are included in this chapter.

GOLDEN "SPUN" SUGAR: Combine ¼ cup sugar and 1 tablespoon corn syrup in a small heavy skillet; heat slowly until sugar melts and turns golden in color. Carefully add 1 tablespoon hot water. Mixture will bubble. Stir with a spoon and cool until syrupy thick and sticky. Use immediately.

BANANA-STRAWBERRY PARFAIT

Makes 6 servings.

- **1 package (3 ounces) strawberry-flavor gelatin**
- **1 ripe banana, mashed**
- **¼ cup sugar**
- **1 tablespoon curaçao**
- **½ cup heavy cream, whipped**

1. Prepare gelatin, following label directions. Pour into an 8x8x2-inch pan. Refrigerate until firm.
2. Combine banana, sugar and curaçao in small saucepan; heat just to boiling. Cool. Fold in whipped cream.
3. Cut gelatin into cubes; alternate with banana sauce in 6 medium-size parfait glasses. Refrigerate until ready to serve.

GLAZED BAKED APPLES

Bake at 350° for 50 minutes.
Makes 6 servings.

- **6 large baking apples**
- **1¼ cups sugar**
- **1¼ cups water**
- **2 tablespoons sugar**

1. Wash and core apples.
2. Pare apples ⅓ down from top; save parings. Place apples in 8-cup shallow baking dish that will just hold apples.
3. Combine the 1¼ cups sugar and water in a medium-size saucepan; add apple parings. Bring to boiling; lower heat. Simmer 10 minutes. Remove parings. Pour syrup over apples.
4. Bake in moderate oven (350°) 50 minutes, or until apples are tender. Remove from oven.
5. Sprinkle tops of apples with remaining 2 tablespoons sugar. Place under broiler (watching carefully) until sugar is bubbly and apples are well glazed. Serve the apples warm or chilled.

BANANAS FOSTER

Makes 4 servings.

- **½ cup firmly packed brown sugar**
- **¼ cup (½ stick) butter or margarine**
- **4 ripe bananas, peeled and quartered**
  Dash of cinnamon
- **½ cup light rum**
- **¼ cup banana liqueur**
- **1 pint vanilla ice cream**

1. Melt brown sugar and butter or margarine in a chafing dish or skillet, stirring often.
2. Add bananas and sauté just until soft (don't overcook). Sprinkle cinnamon over bananas.
3. Heat rum and banana liqueur in a small saucepan. Pour over bananas, but do not stir into sauce. Carefully light liquor in chafing dish and keep spooning sauce over bananas till flames die.
4. Scoop ice cream into 4 large dessert dishes. Spoon bananas and sauce over and serve the dessert immediately.

PEACH MERINGUE CROWN

Bakes twice at 250° for 45 minutes.
Makes 12 servings.

- **6 egg whites**
- **1¾ cups sugar**
- **1 quart vanilla ice cream**
- **3 large ripe peaches, peeled, halved and pitted**
  Almond Peach Glaze (recipe follows)

1. Line a cooky sheet with brown paper; draw a 7-inch circle in center, using a bowl or salad plate as a guide.
2. Make meringue in two batches: Beat 3 egg whites until foamy-white and double in volume in a medium-size bowl. Sprinkle in 1 cup of the sugar very slowly, 1 tablespoon at a time, beating all the time until sugar dissolves completely and meringue stands in firm peaks.
3. Spread mixture inside the outline on brown paper, building up a 2-inch rim around edge.
4. Bake in very slow oven (250°) 45 minutes, or until firm. Let cool on paper while making second batch of meringue.
5. Beat remaining 3 egg whites with remaining ¾ cup sugar, following Steps 2 and 3.

6. Fit a large star tip onto a pastry bag and fill with meringue mixture. Pipe rings around side and on top of baked meringue rim; make swirls around top with remaining meringue.
7. Bake "decorated" meringue in very slow oven (250°) 45 minutes, or until firm. Cool completely on paper, then loosen shell with a spatula. (This can be done several days before serving; simply store meringue shell in a container with a tight-fitting lid.)
8. One hour before serving: Place meringue shell on a serving plate. Scoop ice cream with large spoon to make "petals" and fill meringue shell. Arrange peach halves over ice cream; top with Almond Peach Glaze.

ALMOND PEACH GLAZE: Mash 1 peeled, halved and pitted ripe peach in a small saucepan; stir in ½ cup light corn syrup. Heat to boiling; reduce heat; simmer 5 minutes. Remove from heat; stir in ½ teaspoon almond extract. Cool. Makes about 1 cup.

BAVARIANS, MOUSSES & GELATINS

CATHEDRAL CAKE

Preparation time: 30 minutes.
Makes 10 servings.

- **1 cup boiling water**
- **1 package (3 ounces) lemon-flavor gelatin**
  Ice cubes
  Few drops green food coloring
- **1 package (3 ounces) ladyfingers, split**
- **2 packages (3½ ounces each) strawberry-flavor whipped dessert mix**
- **1 cup very cold milk**
- **1 cup very cold water**
- **1 teaspoon rum extract**
  Frozen whipped topping, thawed

1. Add boiling water to gelatin in a medium-size bowl; stir until dissolved.
2. Add 8 to 10 ice cubes. Stir until mixture thickens, but is not set. Quickly remove any remaining ice particles with a slotted spoon. Pour half the mixture into a loaf pan. Tint remaining mixture with a few drops green food coloring and pour into a second loaf pan. Chill 15 minutes, or until the gelatin has become firm.

3. Line the side of an 8-inch spring-form pan with ladyfingers. Arrange remaining ladyfingers in the bottom of the pan.

4. Prepare dessert mix with milk and water, following label directions; flavor with rum extract. Chill for about 5 minutes.

5. Cut firm gelatin into ½-inch cubes. Reserve a few cubes of each color for garnish. Fold remaining cubes into prepared dessert mix. Spoon mixture into prepared spring-form pan. Chill at least 4 hours.

6. To serve: Run a thin-bladed knife along edge of spring-form pan. Release spring and remove side. Place cake and spring-form bottom on serving plate. Garnish with whipped topping and reserved gelatin cubes.

FROZEN NEAPOLITAN DESSERT

Makes 10 servings.

    2 packages (2 ounces each) whipped topping mix
    1 cup very cold milk
    ½ cup finely chopped candied fruits
    2 tablespoons light rum OR: 1 teaspoon rum extract
      Red food coloring
    1 package (4 ounces) chocolate-flavor whipped dessert mix
    ¾ cup very cold milk
    ⅓ cup chopped, toasted sliced almonds
    1 pint vanilla ice cream
    2 tablespoons green creme de menthe OR: ½ teaspoon mint extract
      Green food coloring
      Candied red cherries
      Toasted sliced almonds

1. Prepare one package of the whipped topping mix with ½ cup of the milk, following label directions. Fold in candied fruits and rum. Tint a pale pink with a few drops red food coloring. Spread mixture to coat inside of an 8-cup melon mold. Freeze while preparing next mixture.

2. Prepare chocolate dessert mix, using ¾ cup very cold milk instead of water and milk as stated in label directions. Beat 3 minutes; fold in almonds. Spread mixture to coat candied fruit layer, leaving a hollow in center; freeze.

3. Stir ice cream in a medium-size bowl until softened; blend in creme de menthe. Tint ice cream a pale green with green food coloring;

spoon into hollow center. Cover mold with plastic wrap. Freeze at least 4 hours.

4. When ready to serve: Prepare remaining package whipped topping mix with remaining ½ cup very cold milk, following label directions. Unmold dessert by dipping in and out of very hot water quickly, then inverting onto serving plate. Frost with prepared topping. Garnish with halved candied cherries and toasted sliced almonds.

RICE IMPERATRICE WITH CHERRY SAUCE

Makes 10 servings.

    ½ cup uncooked regular rice
    2 cups water
  2¼ cups milk
    1 envelope unflavored gelatin
    ¼ cup cold water
    2 eggs
    ½ cup sugar
    1 teaspoon vanilla
    1 cup heavy cream, whipped
      Cherry Sauce (recipe follows)

1. Cook rice in the 2 cups water in a medium-size saucepan, stirring occasionally, 30 minutes, or until all the water is absorbed. Add 1¼ cups of the milk to rice; simmer 30 minutes longer, or until milk is absorbed. Cool.

2. Soften gelatin in cold water.

3. Beat eggs lightly in top of a double boiler; add sugar and remaining milk. Cook over simmering water, stirring constantly, until mixture coats a spoon. Add vanilla and softened gelatin; stir until the gelatin is completely dissolved. Turn into a large bowl; stir in the rice.

4. Chill custard mixture over ice and water, or in refrigerator, stirring often, until mixture starts to thicken. Fold in whipped cream. Turn into a 6-cup mold. Refrigerate 3 hours, or until firm. Unmold on serving plate. Garnish with additional whipped cream and cherries from Cherry Sauce, if you wish. Serve with Cherry Sauce.

CHERRY SAUCE: Reserve a few cherries from a 1 pound, 5 ounce can cherry pie filling for garnish. Turn remaining pie filling into container of electric blender. Whirl until smooth. Stir in 2 tablespoons brandy and a few drops of red food coloring, if you wish. Chill before serving.

CHESTNUT BAVARIAN CREAM

Makes 8 servings.

  1 can (1 pound) chestnuts in light syrup
  ¾ cup sugar
  2 envelopes unflavored gelatin
  ¼ teaspoon salt
  6 egg yolks, slightly beaten
  3 cups milk
  ¼ cup Grand Marnier or orange juice
1½ cups heavy cream

1. Whirl chestnuts and syrup, half at a time, in container of electric blender until finely pureed (or press through a sieve). Reserve.
2. Combine sugar, gelatin and salt in a medium-size heavy saucepan; add egg yolks; beat until well-blended. Stir in milk. Cook, stirring constantly, over medium heat, just until mixture coats a spoon and is slightly thickened (do not let mixture boil). Remove from heat; stir in liqueur or orange juice and chestnut puree.
3. Pour mixture into a large bowl; place in a larger bowl filled with ice and water. Chill, stirring often, until the mixture mounds when spooned.
4. While mixture chills, beat cream until stiff in a medium-size bowl; fold into gelatin mixture. Pour into a 6-cup mold; chill until firm, at least 4 hours, or overnight.
5. Just before serving, loosen bavarian around edge with a knife; dip mold very quickly in and out of hot water. Cover mold with serving plate; turn upside down; shake gently; lift off mold. Garnish with extra whipped cream, orange wedges and green candied cherries, if you wish.

COOL LEMON SOUFFLÉ

Makes 8 servings.

  1 tablespoon grated lemon rind
  ⅔ cup lemon juice
  2 envelopes unflavored gelatin
  ½ cup water
  6 eggs
1½ cups sugar
  2 cups heavy cream

1. Prepare 4-cup soufflé or other straightsided dish with foil collar this way: Measure two lengths of foil long enough to encircle dish.

Fold in half lengthwise (foil should be about 2 inches higher than the rim of the dish). Fasten collar with tape or paper clips.
2. Grate the lemon rind and squeeze the juice; reserve.
3. Sprinkle gelatin over water in a small saucepan. Let stand 10 minutes, until gelatin is softened. Place saucepan over very low heat until gelatin dissolves (mixture will be clear). Remove from heat; cool.
4. Combine eggs and sugar in large bowl. Beat with electric mixer at high speed until very thick and light. (This will take 7 to 8 minutes.)
5. While eggs and sugar are beating, whip 1½ cups of the cream in a small bowl until soft peaks form; refrigerate.
6. Combine lemon rind and juice with cooled gelatin; pour into egg-sugar mixture. Continue beating until well blended.
7. Remove bowl from mixer. Chill briefly (5 minutes) either in refrigerator or by placing bowl in a large bowl partly filled with ice and water. Stir frequently, just until mixture is thick enough to mound.
8. Fold in whipped cream with a rubber scraper until no streaks of white remain. Pour into prepared dish. Refrigerate at least 3 hours, or until set. Remove collar gently, freeing soufflé from foil, if necessary, with a small paring knife.
9. Beat remaining cream; garnish soufflé.

STRAWBERRY CHARLOTTE

Makes 12 servings.

  1 package (3 ounces) ladyfingers
  2 envelopes unflavored gelatin
  ¾ cup sugar
  4 eggs, separated
  1 cup milk
  1 pint strawberries
  3 tablespoons orange juice
  1 cup heavy cream
  ¼ cup red currant jelly
  3 tablespoons finely chopped pistachio nuts
    Candied Strawberries (recipe follows)

1. Split ladyfingers and arrange around the side of an 8-inch spring-form pan. Arrange remaining ladyfingers in bottom of pan.
2. Combine gelatin and ¼ cup of the sugar in a medium-size saucepan. Add egg yolks and

milk. Beat with a wire whip or rotary beater until smooth.

3. Cook, stirring constantly, over low heat, until mixture thickens slightly and coats spoon. Pour into large bowl.

4. Wash and hull strawberries; mash berries in a large bowl and stir into gelatin mixture with orange liqueur or orange juice. Place bowl in a pan partly filled with ice and water to speed setting. Chill, stirring often, until as thick as unbeaten egg white.

5. Beat egg whites until foamy-white and double in volume in a medium-size bowl. Beat in the remaining ½ cup sugar, 1 tablespoon at a time, until meringue stands in soft peaks. Beat cream until stiff in a small bowl.

6. Fold meringue and whipped cream into gelatin mixture until no streaks of white remain.

7. Spoon gelatin mixture into prepared pan. Chill at least 4 hours, or until gelatin is set.

8. Loosen gelatin around edge of pan with a knife; release spring and carefully remove side of pan.

9. Melt jelly in a small saucepan. Brush ladyfingers with jelly and sprinkle with chopped nuts. Garnish center with some of the Candied Strawberries. Serve remainder of the strawberries with dessert.

CANDIED STRAWBERRIES

Makes 1 pint.

1 pint strawberries
¾ cup sugar
¾ cup water

1. Wash strawberries well and dry completely on paper toweling.

2. Combine sugar and water in a small heavy saucepan. Heat to boiling and cook until syrup reaches 260° on a candy thermometer, or until a little syrup dropped into cold water becomes brittle. Remove from heat.

3. Working quickly, pierce 1 strawberry at a time, at the hull end, with a two-tined fork. Dip berry into hot syrup to coat up to the hull. Hold fork over saucepan several seconds to allow excess syrup to drain back into pan. Place berry on a foil-lined cooky sheet until firm.

NOTE: Candied berries are fragile and should, therefore, be made at the last minute.

PEACH BAVARIAN WITH MELBA SAUCE

Makes 10 servings.

2 envelopes unflavored gelatin
¼ cup water
4 eggs, separated
¼ cup sugar
½ teaspoon salt
1 cup milk
1 can (1 pound) cling peach halves
1 teaspoon vanilla
½ teaspoon almond extract
¼ cup sugar
½ cup heavy cream, whipped

Melba Sauce:
1 tablespoon sugar
2 teaspoons cornstarch
1 package (10 ounces) frozen raspberries, thawed
2 tablespoons Kirsch

1. Sprinkle gelatin over water; let stand for 5 minutes.

2. Beat egg yolks slightly in top of double boiler. Stir in sugar, salt, milk and softened gelatin. Cook, stirring constantly, over simmering water until mixture coats a metal spoon.

3. Pour egg yolk-gelatin mixture into a large mixing bowl; place bowl into another bowl containing ice water. Chill, stirring often, until mixture is syrupy.

4. Drain peaches; puree in electric blender. Stir into chilled egg yolk-gelatin mixture. Continue stirring over ice water until mixture is the consistency of unbeaten egg white.

5. Beat egg whites until foamy white; gradually beat in remaining ¼ cup sugar. Beat until meringue forms soft peaks. Fold into egg yolk-gelatin mixture. Fold in whipped cream. Turn into a 7 or 8 cup mold.

6. Refrigerate 4 hours or until firm; unmold on serving plate. Garnish the bavarian with additional peach halves and Melba Sauce, as shown on our cover photograph.

MELBA SAUCE: Combine sugar and cornstarch in saucepan. Add raspberries. Cook, stirring constantly, until mixture thickens and clears. Force mixture through a sieve to remove seeds. Refrigerate. Stir in Kirsch. Spoon over the Peach Bavarian mold.

CHERRY CORDIAL CHOCOLATE SOUFFLÉ

Makes 10 servings.

1 tablespoon brandy or rum
10 maraschino cherries with stems
8 eggs
1 envelope unflavored gelatin
¼ cup water
1 cup milk
½ cup sugar
½ teaspoon salt
8 squares semisweet chocolate
1 teaspoon rum extract
Whipped cream

1. Pour brandy or rum over cherries in a small bowl; place in freezer, turning cherries a few times, 1 hour.
2. Prepare an ungreased 5- or 6-cup soufflé dish this way: Fold a piece of wax paper, 25 inches long, in half lengthwise; wrap around dish to make a 3-inch stand-up collar; hold in place with string and a paper clip.
3. Soften gelatin in water in a cup.
4. Heat milk slowly in a medium-size saucepan until bubbles start to appear around the edge.
5. Separate eggs, putting whites in a large bowl and yolks in a medium-size bowl. Beat yolks slightly with ¼ cup of the sugar. Pour the hot milk into the yolks, beating constantly; return mixture to saucepan.
6. Cook over low heat, stirring constantly, until custard starts to thicken and coats a spoon; remove from heat. Stir in softened gelatin, until melted; add rum extract. Strain back into medium-size bowl.
7. Melt chocolate squares in a small bowl over hot water.
8. Remove cherries from brandy; holding by the stem, dip one at a time into melted chocolate to coat completely. Place on wax paper; refrigerate.
9. Add remaining chocolate and brandy from cherries to yolk mixture; beat until smooth; set bowl in a larger bowl partly filled with ice and water; chill at room temperature, stirring often, just until as thick as unbeaten egg white.
10. While mixture chills, beat egg whites until foamy-white and double in volume. Add remaining ¼ cup sugar, 1 tablespoon at a time, beating until meringue stands in firm peaks.
11. Beat about ¼ of the meringue into thickened chocolate mixture. Fold remaining meringue into chocolate until no streaks of white remain. Spoon into prepared soufflé dish. Chill several hours, or until firm.
12. Just before serving, carefully remove collar; garnish with whipped cream or thawed frozen whipped topping and the chocolate cordial cherries.

MOLDED CANTALOUPE CREAM

Makes 8 servings.

1 package (3 ounces) orange-flavor gelatin
1 cup boiling water
1¾ cups orange juice
¼ teaspoon ground ginger
1 large ripe cantaloupe
2 envelopes unflavored gelatin
½ cup sugar
2 teaspoons grated orange rind
1 package (2 ounces) whipped topping mix
Milk

1. Dissolve orange gelatin in boiling water in a medium-size bowl; stir in ¾ cup of the orange juice and ginger. Cool. Chill until as thick as unbeaten egg white.
2. While orange gelatin mixture chills, halve and seed cantaloupe. Shape 1 cup cantaloupe balls with a melon ball scoop or the ½ teaspoon from your measuring spoon set. Save remaining cantaloupe for Step 4.
3. Fold melon balls into chilled gelatin; pour into a 6-cup mold. Chill just until sticky-firm.
4. Cut remaining cantaloupe into small pieces. Combine with remaining 1 cup orange juice in electric-blender container; cover. Whirl until very smooth. (If you do not have a blender, press cantaloupe through a fine sieve or food mill; stir in orange juice.)
5. Combine unflavored gelatin and sugar in medium-size saucepan; stir in 1 cup of the cantaloupe purée. Heat slowly, stirring constantly, just until gelatin dissolves. Remove from heat. Combine with remaining cantaloupe purée and orange rind in a large bowl. Chill 30 minutes.
6. Prepare whipped topping mix with milk, following label directions. Fold into cantaloupe purée mixture. Pour carefully over gelatin layer in mold. Chill for about 4 hours, or until firm.

7. Just before serving, loosen mold around edge with a knife; dip mold very quickly in and out of hot water. Wipe water off mold. Shake mold gently to loosen. Cover with a serving plate; turn upside down; gently lift off mold. Garnish with fresh mint, if you wish.

STRAWBERRY MOUSSE

Makes 8 servings.

  2 **pints (4 cups) strawberries**
1⅔ **cups sugar**
  ⅛ **teaspoon cream of tartar**
  ⅓ **cup water**
  3 **egg whites**
  2 **cups heavy cream**
  2 **teaspoons cornstarch**
    Few drops red food coloring
    Fondant Strawberries (recipe follows)

1. Save 6 perfect strawberries for garnish. Hull remaining berries; combine with 1 cup of the sugar in a large bowl. Crush with a fork or potato masher. Drain through a sieve, reserving strawberry liquid for sauce. (You should have about 1 cup.)
2. Combine remaining ⅔ cup sugar, cream of tartar and water in a saucepan. Heat slowly, stirring constantly, until sugar is dissolved, then cook rapidly, without stirring, to 240° on a candy thermometer, or until syrup spins a 2-inch thread.
3. While syrup cooks, beat egg whites until they form soft peaks in a large bowl. Pour hot syrup slowly in a thin but steady stream over whites, beating constantly, until meringue stands in firm peaks.
4. Beat heavy cream until stiff in a large bowl. Fold in crushed strawberries, then fold in meringue until no streaks of white remain. Spoon into an 8-cup mold; freeze until firm.
5. To make sauce, combine reserved strawberry liquid and cornstarch until smooth in a small saucepan. Cook, stirring constantly, over medium heat, until mixture thickens and bubbles 1 minute; cool. Refrigerate till ready to use.
6. When ready to serve, run a sharp-tip thin-blade knife around top of mold to loosen; dip mold quickly in and out of hot water. (Be sure water reaches the top of mold.) Cover mold with a plate; turn upside down; lift off mold.

7. Spoon a small amount of sauce over mousse and pass remainder separately. Garnish with Fondant Strawberries.

FONDANT STRAWBERRIES: In top of a double boiler combine 1 cup sifted 10X (confectioners') sugar and 2 tablespoons corn syrup. Cook over simmering, not boiling, water, stirring until melted and smooth; cool slightly. Dip the 6 reserved strawberries half-way into mixture; place on wax paper to set.

CHEESECAKES

SOUR CREAM WALNUT CHEESECAKE

Bake at 350° for 40 minutes, then 5 minutes longer to set topping.
Makes 12 servings.

  1 **cup zwieback crumbs**
  2 **tablespoons sugar (for crust)**
  ¼ **cup chopped walnuts**
  2 **tablespoons butter or margarine, melted**
  2 **packages (8 ounces each) cream cheese, softened**
  ½ **cup sugar**
  1 **teaspoon vanilla**
  3 **eggs, well beaten**
  1 **cup dairy sour cream**
  ½ **teaspoon vanilla**
  1 **tablespoon sugar (for topping)**

1. Combine zwieback crumbs, 2 tablespoons sugar and 2 tablespoons of the walnuts; blend in butter or margarine. Press evenly on bottom and side of an 8-inch spring-form pan. Chill.
2. Beat cream cheese in large bowl of electric mixer at medium speed until fluffy. Gradually beat in sugar and 1 teaspoon of the vanilla. Beat in eggs, a third at a time. Turn into pan.
3. Bake in moderate oven (350°) 40 minutes, or until center is firm. Remove from oven. Cool on wire rack 5 minutes, away from drafts.
4. Combine sour cream, remaining 1 tablespoon sugar and vanilla. Spread over top of cake; sprinkle with remaining walnuts.
5. Return to moderate oven (350°) for 5 minutes, or until topping is set. Remove from oven; cool in pan on wire rack, away from drafts. Remove side of pan. Refrigerate for 4 hours.

UPSIDE-DOWN ORANGE CHEESECAKE

It's easy to have a refreshing orange topping on this cheesecake—just make it upside down. Makes 10 servings.

    2 envelopes unflavored gelatin
1½ cups orange juice
    1 cup sugar
    1 orange, thinly sliced
    3 eggs, separated
    1 tablespoon grated orange rind
    2 tablespoons orange flavored liqueur
    3 containers (8 ounces each) cottage cheese
½ cup dairy sour cream
    1 cup vanilla wafer crumbs
½ teaspoon ground cinnamon
    3 tablespoons butter or margarine, melted

1. Soften 1 teaspoon of the gelatin in ¾ cup of the orange juice 5 minutes; stir in ½ cup of the sugar. Heat, stirring constantly, over medium heat, until gelatin melts. Chill until mixture is syrupy-thick.
2. Arrange orange slices in a 9x9x2-inch pan, as pictured on page 114. Pour syrupy orange juice over. Chill.
3. Soften remaining gelatin in remaining juice 5 minutes in a small pan. Heat, stirring constantly, until just below the boiling point. Beat egg yolks slightly in a small bowl. Slowly add half of hot gelatin mixture; stir back into pan. Cook, stirring constantly, until mixture thickens slightly. (Do not allow to boil.) Remove from heat; stir in orange rind and orange liqueur.
4. Combine half of cottage cheese, half of sour cream and half of gelatin mixture in container of electric blender. Whirl at high speed until smooth and completely blended. Pour into large bowl. Repeat with remaining cheese, sour cream and gelatin mixture. Chill, stirring often, until mixture mounds slightly when spooned.
5. Beat egg whites until foamy-white and double in volume in a small bowl. Beat in remaining sugar, 1 tablespoon at a time, until meringue stands in firm peaks. Fold meringue into cottage cheese mixture. Pour over orange layer in pan. Chill at least 4 hours, or until firm.
6. Combine crumbs with cinnamon in small bowl; blend in butter or margarine. Spread over top of cheesecake and press down firmly with hands. Chill briefly to set crumb layer.
7. Loosen cake around edge with a small spatula; dip pan quickly in and out of hot water. Place serving plate over pan, turn upside down; shake pan gently to release cake; lift off pan. Keep refrigerated until serving time.

FAMILY CIRCLE'S BEST CHEESECAKE

Bake at 475° for 10 minutes, then at 200° for 1 hour.
Makes 16 servings.

    1 cup graham-cracker crumbs (from a 13½-ounce package)
    1 tablespoon sugar (for crust)
½ teaspoon ground cinnamon
    1 tablespoon butter or margarine, melted (for crust)
    5 packages (8 ounces each) cream cheese
1¾ cups sugar (for cake)
    3 tablespoons flour
1½ teaspoons grated orange rind
    5 eggs
    2 egg yolks
¼ cup milk
    Orange Glaze (recipe follows)

1. Combine graham-cracker crumbs, 1 tablespoon sugar and cinnamon in a small bowl; blend in the melted butter or margarine. Press firmly over bottom of a lightly greased 9-inch spring-form pan. Chill briefly before filling.
2. Let cream cheese soften in a large bowl; blend in sugar, flour and orange rind. Beat with electric mixer until light and fluffy. Add eggs and egg yolks, one at a time, beating well after each; stir in milk; pour into crumb crust.
3. Bake in hot oven (475°) 10 minutes; lower temperature to 200° and bake 1 hour longer; let cake remain in oven until cool (1 hour).
4. Remove from oven; cool completely on a wire rack; loosen around edge with a knife; release spring and remove side of pan. Top with Orange Glaze.

ORANGE GLAZE: Drain the syrup from an 11-ounce jar mandarin oranges; reserve ½ cup syrup. Combine 2 teaspoons cornstarch and 1 teaspoon sugar in a small saucepan. Slowly stir in reserved syrup; cook, stirring constantly, over medium heat, until mixture thickens and bubbles 1 minute; cool. Dip the orange slices in the glaze before placing them on the cake.

Cool Lemon Soufflé offers elegance and ease in
one big, beautiful serving bowl. Recipe is included
in this chapter.

Fabulous cheesecake recipes in this chapter
include ones for (going clockwise, from top left):
Pineapple Cheesecake, Welsh Cheddar Cheesecake,
Frozen Blueberry Ripple Cheesecake, Lattice Cherry Cheese Pie,
Upside-Down Orange Cheesecake, Sour Cream Walnut
Cheesecake and Ricotta Cheese Pie.

Top: Peach Meringue Crown. The recipes for all the desserts shown here are in this chapter.
Chocolate Floating Islands   Mocha Walnut Torte   Molded Cantaloupe Cream

RICOTTA CHEESE PIE

Bake at 350° for 1 hour.
Makes 8 servings.

1½ containers (15 ounces each) ricotta cheese
1⅓ cups sugar
  1 tablespoon flour
  4 eggs, slightly beaten
  1 teaspoon vanilla
  3 tablespoons semisweet chocolate pieces, coarsely chopped
  3 tablespoons candied citron, chopped
  3 tablespoons candied orange peel, chopped
  1 recipe Cooky Crust (recipe follows)

1. Roll out half the Cooky Crust dough to a 12-inch round on a lightly floured pastry board; fit into a 9-inch pie plate; trim overhang to ½-inch.
2. Reserve 2 tablespoons egg for brushing pastry later. Combine ricotta cheese, sugar and flour in electric mixer; beat until smooth. Add eggs and vanilla; beat until light and fluffy. Stir in chocolate, citron and orange peel; spoon into prepared pie shell.
3. Roll out remaining Cooky Crust dough to a 12x8-inch rectangle, cut lengthwise into 10 strips with a pastry wheel or knife. Weave strips over filling to make a crisscross top; trim overhang to ½ inch; turn under, flush with rim; flute edge. Mix reserved egg with 1 tablespoon water; brush pastry.
4. Bake in moderate oven (350°) for 1 hour, or until pastry is golden and filling is firm. Cool on wire rack. Sprinkle pie with 10X (confectioners') sugar and chocolate curls, if you wish. NOTE: Check pie after about ½ hour. If edges seem to be getting too brown, cover with foil for remainder of baking time.

COOKY CRUST

  2 cups sifted all-purpose flour
  ½ cup sugar
  ¾ cup (1½ sticks) butter or margarine, softened
  2 egg yolks, slightly beaten
  1 teaspoon vanilla

Mix flour and sugar together in a medium-size bowl; cut in butter or margarine with a pastry blender until mixture is crumbly. Add egg yolks and vanilla; mix lightly with a fork just until pastry holds together and leaves sides of bowl clean. Chill until ready to use.
NOTE: For half the recipe, use 1 cup flour, ¼ cup sugar, 6 tablespoons butter or margarine, 1 egg yolk and ½ teaspoon vanilla.

FROZEN BLUEBERRY RIPPLE CHEESECAKE

Makes 12 servings.

  ¾ cup graham cracker crumbs
  2 tablespoons sugar
  3 tablespoons butter or margarine, melted
  1 cup sugar
  ⅓ cup water
  ⅛ teaspoon cream of tartar
  3 egg whites
  2 packages (8 ounces each) cream cheese
  ½ cup dairy sour cream
  2 teaspoons vanilla
  1 tablespoon grated lemon rind
  ½ cup blueberry preserves
    Whipped cream
    Fresh or frozen unsweetened blueberries

1. Combine crumbs, sugar and butter or margarine in a small bowl; blend well. Press firmly over bottom of an 8-inch spring-form pan. Chill.
2. Combine sugar, water and cream of tartar in a small saucepan; bring to boiling. Boil rapidly 8 to 10 minutes, or until syrup registers 236° on a candy thermometer (or until syrup spins a 2-inch thread when dropped from spoon).
3. Meanwhile in large bowl of electric mixer, beat egg whites until stiff peaks form; pour hot syrup in a thin stream over egg whites while beating constantly. Continue beating until very stiff peaks form and mixture cools, altogether about 15 minutes.
4. Beat cream cheese and sour cream until light and fluffy; beat in vanilla and lemon rind. Add ¼ of meringue to cheese mixture; stir to combine well. Fold remaining meringue into cheese mixture until no streaks of meringue and cheese remain.
5. Spoon about ¼ of cheese mixture into prepared pan; drizzle part of blueberry preserves over. Continue to layer cheese mixture and preserves this way. Freeze overnight, or until firm.
6. Decorate cheesecake with whipped cream and fresh or frozen unsweetened blueberries.

WELSH CHEDDAR CHEESECAKE

Bake at 475° for 12 minutes, then at 250° for
1½ hours.
Makes 16 servings.

  1 box (6 ounces) zwieback crackers, crushed
  3 tablespoons sugar (for crust)
  6 tablespoons (¾ stick) butter or margarine,
    melted
  4 packages (8 ounces each) cream cheese
  8 ounces finely shredded Cheddar cheese (2
    cups)
1¾ cups sugar
  3 tablespoons flour
  5 eggs
  3 egg yolks
  ¼ cup beer

1. Combine the zwieback crumbs, 3 tablespoons
sugar and melted butter or margarine in a small
bowl. Press firmly over the bottom and partly
up the sides of a lightly buttered 9-inch spring-
form pan. Chill briefly before filling.
2. Let cream cheese soften in a large bowl. Beat
with Cheddar cheese, just until smooth.
(Cheeses will beat smoother if they are at room
temperature.) Add sugar and flour. Beat until
light and fluffy. Add eggs and egg yolks, one at
a time, beating well after each addition; stir in
beer; pour into crumb crust.
3. Bake in very hot oven (475°) 12 minutes;
lower temperature to 250° and bake 1½ hours
longer. Turn off oven; let cake remain in oven
for an hour.
4. Remove from oven; cool completely on a
wire rack; loosen around edge with a knife; release spring and remove side of pan.
NOTE: It is the nature of this cake to crack on
top. However, this will not affect its flavor.

PINEAPPLE CHEESECAKE

Bake at 475° for 12 minutes, then at 250° for
1½ hours.
Makes 16 servings.

  ½ recipe Cooky Crust (recipe, page 117)
    Pineapple Filling, (recipe follows)
  5 packages (8 ounces each) cream cheese
1¾ cups sugar
  3 tablespoons flour
  1 teaspoon vanilla

  5 eggs
  2 egg yolks
  ¼ cup heavy cream

1. Roll ⅓ of chilled Cooky Crust dough to cover
the bottom of a 10-inch spring-form pan.
2. Bake in hot oven (400°) for 8 minutes, or
until crust is lightly browned; cool. Butter sides
of the spring-form pan; roll remaining dough
into 2 strips about 15 inches long and 2½ inches
wide; press onto sides of pan and fit together
with bottom. Refrigerate.
3. Let cream cheese soften in a large bowl;
blend in sugar, flour and vanilla. Beat with electric mixer until light and fluffy. Add eggs and
egg yolks, one at a time, beating well after each
addition; stir in heavy cream; spoon Pineapple
Filling into crust; pour cheese mixture over.
4. Bake in a very hot oven (475°) 12 minutes;
lower temperature to 250° and bake 1½ hours.
Turn off oven; let cake remain in oven 1 hour.
5. Remove from oven; cool on a wire rack;
loosen around edge with a knife; release spring
and remove side of pan.

PINEAPPLE FILLING: Combine 3 tablespoons
sugar and 1 tablespoon cornstarch in a small
saucepan. Slowly stir in contents of a 1 pound,
4 ounce can of crushed pineapple. Cook, stirring constantly, over medium heat, until mixture
thickens and bubbles 1 minute; cool.

LATTICE CHERRY-CHEESE PIE

Bake at 350° for 30 minutes, then at 450° for
10 minutes.
Makes 8 servings.

  ½ recipe Cooky Crust (recipe on page 117)
  4 packages (3 ounces each) cream cheese
  1 container (8 ounces) cottage cheese
  ¾ cup sugar
  1 teaspoon vanilla
  ⅛ teaspoon ground nutmeg
  2 eggs
  ¼ teaspoon ground cinnamon
  1 can (1 pound, 5 ounces) cherry pie filling

1. Roll out Cooky Crust dough to an 11-inch
round on floured surface, or between 2 sheets
of wax paper; fit into a 9-inch pie plate. Trim
overhang to ½ inch; turn under, flush with rim.

2. Combine 3 packages of the cream cheese and cottage cheese in medium-size bowl; beat with electric beater until smooth; beat in sugar, vanilla and nutmeg. Add eggs, one at a time, beating well after each; measure out ⅓ cup of mixture; set aside. Pour remaining cheese mixture into prepared pie shell.

3. Bake in moderate oven (350°) 30 minutes. Meanwhile, combine reserved cheese mixture and remaining 1 package cream cheese in bowl; beat until smooth. Fit a pastry bag with a plain round tip (about ¼ inch in diameter); fill with cream-cheese mixture. Stir cinnamon into cherry pie filling.

4. Remove pie from oven; turn oven temperature to 450°. Spread cherry filling over top of pie. Pipe cheese mixture over pie in a lattice pattern and around edge. Bake in very hot oven (450°) 10 minutes longer, or until lattice is nicely browned. Cool completely on wire rack. Serve at room temperature.

ECLAIRS & CREAM PUFFS

ECLAIRS

Bake at 400° for 25 minutes.
Makes 3 dozen.

  1 cup water
  ½ cup (1 stick) butter or margarine
  1 cup sifted all-purpose flour
  ¼ teaspoon salt
  4 eggs
  Almond Filling (recipe follows)
  2 cups sifted 10X (confectioners') sugar
  3 tablespoons freshly brewed strong coffee
  3 squares unsweetened chocolate

1. Heat water and butter or margarine to boiling in a medium-size heavy saucepan. Add flour and salt all at once; stir vigorously with a wooden spoon until mixture forms a thick smooth ball that follows spoon around pan; remove from heat at once.

2. Beat in eggs, one at a time, until shiny-smooth.

3. Attach a plain round tip to a pastry bag; fill with batter. Press out into thin strips, 3 inches long and 1 inch apart, onto cooky sheets.

4. Bake in hot oven (400°) 25 minutes, or until puffed and lightly golden. Remove carefully from cooky sheets to wire racks; cool.

5. Cut a thin slice lengthwise from top of each eclair; lift off. Spoon 1 rounded tablespoonful Almond Filling into each eclair; replace tops.

6. Beat 10X sugar with coffee until smooth in a small bowl; spread over eclairs to glaze lightly; let stand until glaze is firm.

7. Melt chocolate in a cup over hot water; drizzle in ribbons over coffee glaze. Chill until serving time.

ALMOND FILLING

Bake at 350° for 12 minutes.
Makes enough to fill 3 dozen tiny eclairs.

  ½ cup sliced blanched almonds
  ½ cup sugar (for almond candy)
  2 tablespoons water
  ⅔ cup sugar (for filling)
  4 tablespoons cornstarch
  3 tablespoons flour
  ½ teaspoon salt
2½ cups milk
  2 egg yolks
  2 tablespoons butter or margarine
1½ teaspoons vanilla

1. Spread almonds in a shallow baking pan. Toast in moderate oven (350°), shaking pan several times, 12 minutes, or until lightly browned.

2. Combine the ½ cup sugar and water in a medium-size saucepan; heat slowly, stirring constantly, until sugar melts and mixture turns golden. Quickly stir in almonds until coated.

3. Spread at once on a buttered cooky sheet; let stand until firm. Break mixture into small pieces; place in a transparent bag; crush to powder with a rolling pin. Set aside for Step 6.

4. Combine the ⅔ cup sugar, cornstarch, flour and salt in a large saucepan; stir in milk. Cook slowly, stirring constantly, until mixture thickens and bubbles 1 minute.

5. Beat egg yolks slightly in a small bowl; slowly stir in ½ cup of the hot mixture; stir back into remaining mixture in saucepan. Cook, stirring constantly, 3 minutes; remove from heat.

6. Stir in butter or margarine and vanilla; cool. Stir in almond powder; chill.

VIENNESE MOCHA-NUT CROWN

Bake at 400° for 40 minutes.
Makes 6 servings.

  ½ **recipe Basic Cream Puff Paste (page 121)**
Chocolate Praline Filling:
  ½ **cup hazelnuts or almonds, unblanched**
  ⅓ **cup granulated sugar**
  ⅓ **cup water**
  2 **cups heavy cream**
  ⅓ **cup dry cocoa (not a mix)**
  ½ **cup 10X (confectioners') sugar**
    Chocolate Icing (recipe follows)
    Coffee Butter Cream (recipe follows)

1. Make Basic Cream Puff Paste. Draw a 7-inch circle on an ungreased cooky sheet, using a saucer or lid as a guide. Spoon paste in 6 mounds, spacing evenly, just inside circle. Puffs should almost touch. Or, press paste through a pastry bag.
2. Bake in a hot oven (400°) 40 minutes, or until puffed and golden brown. With a small knife, make small slits in ring to let steam escape. Turn off heat; leave ring in oven 5 minutes longer. Remove to wire rack; cool completely.
3. Make Chocolate Praline Filling: Combine nuts, sugar and water in a small heavy skillet. Bring to boiling, stirring constantly. Boil rapidly, uncovered, until nuts make a popping sound, about 10 minutes. Remove from heat; stir with a wooden spoon until sugar crystallizes and becomes dry. Return to pan to heat; cook over low heat just until sugar starts to melt and form a glaze on nuts. Turn out on a cooky sheet; separate with a fork; cool completely. Crush with a rolling pin, or whirl in a blender until almost powdery. Beat cream with cocoa and 10X sugar until stiff in a large bowl; fold in crushed nuts; chill.
4. To assemble: Split ring in half horizontally. Scoop out any filaments of soft dough.
5. Place bottom half of ring on serving plate. Fill with Chocolate Praline Filling. Place top of ring in place. Spoon Chocolate Icing over each puff. Decorate top wih small rosettes of Coffee Butter Cream. Garnish with whole nuts, if you wish. Refrigerate 1 hour, or until ready to serve.

CHOCOLATE ICING: Combine 1 square unsweetened chocolate, 1 tablespoon butter or margarine, 2 teaspoons brandy and 1 tablespoon water in a small bowl. Place in a pan of simmering water, stirring occasionally until chocolate is melted. Remove from heat; stir in ½ cup 10X (confectioners') sugar. (If icing is too thick, add more hot water.) Keep warm.

COFFEE BUTTER CREAM: Dissolve ¼ teaspoon instant coffee in ½ teaspoon water in a small bowl. Add 1 tablespoon soft butter or margarine and ¼ cup 10X (confectioners') sugar. Beat with a fork until smooth. Spoon into a cake decorator fitted with a small star tip.

PEACH DUMPLINGS

Bake at 425° for 30 minutes.
Makes 6 servings.

  ¾ **cup water**
  ½ **cup granulated sugar (for syrup)**
  ¼ **cup bottled grenadine syrup**
  1 **package piecrust mix**
  ¼ **cup firmly packed brown sugar**
  ¼ **teaspoon ground cinnamon**
  1 **tablespoon butter or margarine**
  6 **large peaches, peeled, halved and pitted**
    Milk
    Granulated sugar (for topping)

1. Combine water, the ½ cup granulated sugar and grenadine syrup in a medium-size saucepan. Heat to boiling, then simmer 5 minutes; remove from heat.
2. Prepare piecrust mix, following label directions, or make pastry from your favorite two-crust recipe. Roll out on a lightly floured pastry cloth or board to a rectangle, 18x12; cut into 6 six-inch squares.
3. Blend brown sugar, cinnamon and butter or margarine in a small bowl. Spoon into hollows in the peach halves; press each 2 halves back together.
4. Place a filled peach in center of each pastry square; fold pastry up and around fruit; pinch edges to seal. Place in a baking pan, 13x9x2; pour syrup into pan. Brush dumplings lightly with milk; sprinkle with granulated sugar.
5. Bake in hot oven (425°) 30 minutes, or until pastry is golden and peaches are tender. (Test fruit with a long thin metal skewer.)
6. Cool slightly in pan on a wire rack. Serve warm, with cream or ice cream, if you wish.

BASIC CREAM PUFF PASTE

Makes 12 large cream puffs or 12 large eclairs or 36 miniature cream puffs (profiteroles).

    1   cup water
    ½   cup (1 stick) butter or margarine
    1   teaspoon sugar
    ¼   teaspoon salt
    1   cup sifted all-purpose flour
    4   eggs

1. Heat water, butter or margarine, sugar and salt to a full rolling boil in a large saucepan.
2. Add flour all at once. Stir vigorously with a wooden spoon until mixture forms a thick smooth ball that leaves sides of pan clean (about 1 minute). Remove from heat; cool slightly.
3. Add eggs, one at a time, beating well after each addition until paste is shiny-smooth. Paste will separate as you add each egg, but with continued beating it will smooth out.
4. Shape, following instructions with recipe of your choice.

STRAWBERRY SHORTCAKE SEVILLE

Bake at 425° for 25 minutes.
Makes 8 to 10 servings.

    1   pint strawberries
    ⅓   cup sugar
    2   cups biscuit mix
    ⅔   cup milk
    1   tablespoon grated orange rind
    1   cup heavy cream
    2   teaspoons vanilla

1. Wash strawberries, hull and slice into a medium-size bowl; sprinkle with 2 tablespoons of the sugar; toss lightly to mix. Let stand.
2. Prepare biscuit mix with milk, following label directions for rolled biscuits. Roll out to a 16x12-inch rectangle on a lightly floured pastry board.
3. Mix remaining sugar and orange rind in a cup; sprinkle half over dough; roll up, jelly-roll fashion. Cut into 16 one-inch-thick slices. Place, cut side down, in an 8x8x2-inch greased baking pan, to make 4 rows of 4 biscuits each.
4. Bake in hot oven (425°) 25 minutes.
5. Combine cream and vanilla; beat until stiff.
6. Remove biscuits from pan by turning upside down on a wire rack so as not to break layers. Top with the berries and whipped cream.

STRAWBERRY CHANTILLY TORTE

Bake at 350° for 30 minutes.
Makes 8 to 10 servings.

    1   cup sifted cake flour
    1   teaspoon baking powder
    ¼   teaspoon salt
    ½   cup (1 stick) butter or margarine
    1½ cups sugar
    5   eggs, separated
    1   teaspoon vanilla
    3   tablespoons milk
    ¾   teaspoon almond extract
    ½   cup toasted slivered almonds (from a
        5-ounce can)
    2   pints strawberries
    2   cups heavy cream

1. Butter bottoms of 2 nine-inch layer-cake pans; dust lightly with flour, tapping out any excess.
2. Sift flour, baking powder and salt onto waxed paper.
3. Cream butter or margarine with ½ cup of the sugar until fluffy in a medium-size bowl; beat in egg yolks, one at a time, until blended, then beat in vanilla and milk.
4. Fold in flour mixture until blended; spread evenly in prepared pans.
5. Beat egg whites with ¼ teaspoon of the almond extract until foamy-white and double in volume in a large bowl; sprinkle in ¾ cup of the remaining sugar, 1 tablespoon at a time, beating all the time until sugar dissolves completely and meringue stands in firm peaks. Spread evenly over batter in pans; sprinkle with almonds.
6. Bake in moderate oven (350°) 30 minutes, or until meringue is delicately browned.
7. Cool layers in pans on wire racks 5 minutes; loosen around edges with a knife; turn each out onto palm of hand, then place, meringue side up, on racks; cool completely.
8. Wash strawberries, hull and quarter.
9. Beat cream with remaining ¼ cup sugar and ½ teaspoon almond extract until stiff in a medium-size bowl.
10. Place 1 cake layer on a large serving plate; top with about half of the whipped cream and strawberries. Repeat with second cake layer and remaining strawberries and whipped cream. Cut cake into 8 to 10 wedges with a sharp knife.

EXTRA SPECIALS

APPLE-NUT STRUDEL

Bake at 400° for 50 minutes.
Makes 8 servings.

    3 cups sifted all-purpose flour
    ¼ teaspoon salt
    1 egg
    ¾ cup lukewarm water
    2 tablespoons vegetable oil
    ½ cup (1 stick) butter or margarine, melted
    3 cups soft white bread crumbs (6 slices)
    1 can (1 pound, 4 ounces) pie-sliced apples,
      drained
    ¾ cup raisins
    ½ cup chopped walnuts
    ¾ cup sugar
    1 teaspoon ground cinnamon
      10X (confectioners') sugar

1. Sift flour and salt into a large bowl. Make a well in center of flour and add egg, water and vegetable oil. Stir to make a sticky dough.
2. Place dough on a lightly floured pastry board. Slap dough down onto board, pick up; slap down again for 10 minutes to develop the gluten (as in bread), which gives the elasticity necessary for stretching the dough. Cover dough with a bowl and allow to rest 30 minutes.
3. Place a clean fabric cloth or sheet on a kitchen or card table about 30 inches square. Sprinkle cloth with flour and rub in.
4. Roll out dough to as large a square as possible on floured cloth. Place hands, palm-side down, under dough and begin, gently, to stretch dough, moving around table until dough has stretched over all corners of the table. (Note: Please remove rings and your watch to prevent holes in the dough.)
5. Sprinkle dough with about 2 tablespoons of the melted butter or margarine. Measure two more tablespoons of the melted butter into a large skillet. Add bread crumbs and stir until crumbs have turned a crisp golden brown. Sprinkle crumbs over entire surface of dough.
6. Combine apples, raisins, nuts, sugar and cinnamon in a large bowl. Spoon apple mixture in an even row down one end of dough, 2 inches in from the end.
7. Trim off thick parts of dough on all four

of the overhanging sides with kitchen scissors.
8. Using the overhanging cloth to lift dough, roll dough over filling. Fold the two parallel sides of dough toward center to completely enclose the filling.
9. Lift the cloth at filling end to allow dough to roll over and over until completely rolled.
10. Line a large cooky sheet with a double thickness of heavy duty aluminum foil. Ease filled roll onto cooky sheet, shaping roll into a horseshoe shape. Turn up ends of foil 1 inch all around cooky sheet, to keep oven clean, in case of spill-over.
11. Bake in hot oven (400°) 50 minutes, brushing several times with remaining butter, or until pastry is golden.
12. Allow pastry to cool 15 minutes; slide onto serving board. Sprinkle with 10X sugar.

CHERRY KUCHEN

Bake at 375° for 20 minutes, then 20 minutes longer.
Makes 12 servings.

    ½ cup milk
    2 tablespoons sugar
    1 teaspoon salt
    2 tablespoons shortening
    1 envelope active dry yeast
    ¼ cup very warm water
    1 egg
    2 cups sifted all-purpose flour
    1 can (1 pound, 5 ounces) cherry pie filling
    ¾ cup sugar
    1 teaspoon ground cinnamon
    ¼ teaspoon ground mace
    2 tablespoons butter or margarine, softened
    1 egg, slightly beaten
    ⅓ cup light cream

1. Combine milk, the 2 tablespoons sugar, salt and shortening in a saucepan. Heat until bubbles appear around edge and shortening is melted; cool to lukewarm.
2. Sprinkle yeast into very warm water in a large bowl. ("Very warm" water should feel comfortably warm when dropped on wrist.) Stir until yeast dissolves. Stir in cooled milk mixture and egg. Beat in flour gradually. Cover with a damp towel; let rise in a warm place, away from draft, 45 to 60 minutes, or until it

is exactly double in bulk. Stir the dough down.
3. Spread in greased 13x9x2-inch pan. Spoon cherry pie filling evenly over dough. Mix the ¾ cup sugar with cinnamon, mace and butter. Sprinkle all but 2 tablespoons over cherries. Cover with towel; let rise in a warm place, away from draft, 30 minutes, or until double in bulk.
4. Bake in moderate oven (375°) 20 minutes, or until golden. Mix beaten egg and cream; pour over kuchen; sprinkle with reserved sugar mixture. Bake 20 minutes longer. Serve warm.
NOTE: Experienced bakers have favorite places for raising the dough. One of the best places is in the oven. The heat from the pilot is enough in a gas oven; heat electric to 200°; turn off.

MOCHA WALNUT TORTE

Bake at 350° for 30 minutes.
Makes 12 servings.

2½ cups sifted cake flour
1⅔ cups sugar
3 teaspoons baking powder
1 teaspoon salt
⅔ cup shortening
1¼ cups milk
6 egg yolks
2 teaspoons vanilla
¾ cup apricot preserves
Mocha Frosting (recipe follows)
Walnut Brittle (recipe follows)

1. Grease 2 nine-inch round layer-cake pans; dust lightly with flour; tap out any excess.
2. Sift flour, sugar, baking powder and salt into large bowl of electric mixer. Add shortening and 1 cup of the milk. Beat at medium speed 2 minutes. Add remaining ¼ cup milk, egg yolks and vanilla. Beat at medium speed 2 minutes longer. Pour into prepared pans, spreading evenly.
3. Bake in moderate oven (350°) 30 minutes, or until centers spring back when lightly pressed with fingertip. Cool in pans on wire racks 10 minutes. Loosen layers around edges with a knife; turn out onto racks; cool completely. Split each layer, using a sawing motion with a very sharp knife.
4. Place one split cake layer on serving plate. Spread with ¼ cup of the apricot preserves and ½ of the Mocha Frosting; repeat with 2 more layers, spreading with preserves and frosting,

ending with a plain layer on top. Frost top layer, reserving part of the Mocha Frosting for garnish. Sprinkle Walnut Brittle over top of cake. Fit a pastry bag with a small star tip; fill bag with remaining frosting and garnish cake in middle and around edge with rosettes.

MOCHA FROSTING

Makes enough frosting for 1 four-layer torte

½ cup (1 stick) butter or margarine, softened
1 package 10X (confectioners') sugar, sifted
1 tablespoon instant coffee
3 tablespoons coffee liqueur
2 tablespoons milk

Cream butter or margarine and part of the sugar. Combine coffee, coffee liqueur and milk in a cup. Add alternately with remaining sugar to creamed mixture, beating until frosting is smooth and creamy.

WALNUT BRITTLE: Spread ¾ cup granulated sugar in a small heavy skillet; heat slowly until sugar melts and starts to turn pale golden in color. Stir in ½ cup chopped walnuts and immediately pour out onto a cooky sheet, spreading evenly. Cool completely. Break into small pieces. Makes about 1 cup.

IRISH COFFEE PARFAIT

Makes 8 servings.

2 envelopes unflavored gelatin
½ cup sugar (for coffee)
3½ cups boiling strong brewed coffee
⅓ cup Irish whiskey
1 cup heavy cream
2 tablespoons sugar (for cream)

1. Combine gelatin and the ½ cup sugar in a medium-size bowl. Stir in boiling coffee until sugar and gelatin dissolve. Stir in Irish whiskey.
2. Chill until gelatin is as thick as unbeaten egg whites. Pour gelatin mixture into 8 parfait or dessert glasses. Chill 2 hours, or until gelatin is firm.
3. Beat cream and 2 tablespoons sugar, until stiff in a small bowl. Spoon cream on top of coffee gelatin. Serve the parfait immediately.

PETITS BABAS AU RHUM

Bake at 425° for 8 to 10 minutes.
Makes 4 dozen.

½ cup milk
2 tablespoons sugar
⅛ teaspoon salt
½ cup (1 stick) butter or margarine
1 envelope active dry yeast
¼ cup water
2 eggs
2 cups sifted all-purpose flour
3 tablespoons dried currants
    Rum Syrup (recipe follows)
    Candied red cherries
    Angelica

1. Combine milk, sugar, salt and butter or margarine in a small saucepan. Heat slowly, until butter or margarine melts; cool to lukewarm.
2. Sprinkle yeast into very warm water in a large bowl. ("Very warm water" should feel comfortably warm when dropped on wrist.) Stir until yeast dissolves; stir in milk mixture.
3. Beat in eggs and flour to make a very soft dough. Beat vigorously with a wooden spoon at least 5 minutes, or until dough is very shiny and elastic. Scrape dough down from sides of bowl. Cover with plastic wrap. Let rise in a warm place, away from draft, 45 minutes, or until double in bulk.
4. Beat dough well; stir in currants.
5. Spoon into greased tiny muffin-pan cups, about 1¾ inches across, placing a scant tablespoon in each. (If you do not have enough pans to bake all cakes at once, cover dough and refrigerate while first batch rises and bakes, then stir down before spooning into pans.) Cover; let rise in a warm place, away from draft, 45 minutes, or until almost triple in bulk.
6. Bake in hot oven (425°) 8 to 10 minutes, or until a rich brown. Remove from pans; place, top side down, in one layer in a jelly-roll pan.
7. Pour warm Rum Syrup over while Babas are still warm, then keep basting until all syrup is absorbed. Garnish each Baba Au Rhum with a half candied red cherry and slivers of angelica, or green cherries, if you wish.

RUM SYRUP: Combine 1 cup sugar, 2 cups water and 1 jar (12 ounces) apricot preserves in a medium-size saucepan. Heat to boiling, stirring constantly; reduce heat; simmer, uncovered, 5 minutes. Press through a sieve. Cool 15 minutes; stir in ¾ to 1 cup golden rum to taste. Makes 4 cups.

CHOCOLATE FLOATING ISLANDS

Makes 8 servings.

4 cups milk
6 eggs, separated
2 cups sugar
⅔ cup dry cocoa (not cocoa mix)
2 teaspoons rum extract
½ teaspoon ground nutmeg
    Golden Sugar Ribbons (recipe follows)

1. Heat milk just to simmering over low heat in a large skillet with a cover.
2. Beat egg whites until foamy-white and double in volume in a large bowl. Beat in 1⅓ cups of the sugar, 1 tablespoon at a time, until meringue stands in firm peaks when the beater is lifted.
3. Scoop meringue into egg-shaped puffs with an ice cream scoop or a large spoon, making 4 at a time. Float first 4 puffs, not touching, on simmering milk; cover. Simmer over very low heat 5 minutes.
4. Lift meringue puffs from milk with a slotted spoon; drain on a cooky sheet covered with paper toweling; chill. Repeat, making last 4 puffs with remaining meringue; remove skillet from heat.
5. To make custard sauce: Beat egg yolks until thick in a large bowl; gradually add remaining ⅔ cup sugar. Beat in cocoa and nutmeg until well-blended. Strain milk from skillet into egg-yolk mixture, beating until well-blended.
6. Return cocoa mixture to skillet; cook, stirring constantly, over low heat, until custard thickens slightly and coats spoon. Immediately pour into a bowl. Stir in rum extract; chill.
7. An hour before serving, pour custard sauce into a large shallow glass bowl. Float meringues gently on top; drizzle with Golden Sugar Ribbons. Chill until ready to serve.

GOLDEN SUGAR RIBBONS: Spread ½ cup sugar in a small heavy skillet; heat slowly until sugar melts and starts to turn pale golden in color. Use immediately on floating islands.

Luscious Low-Calorie Creations/9

Low-calorie desserts do not have to be low in appeal, as the recipes in this chapter prove. Look at the picture on the next page and you'll see what we mean. This strawberry cheese pie will help tempt dieting dessert lovers away from the classic cheesecake—its calorie-laden cousin. If you're not on a diet, try our low-calorie creations anyway. They'll watch your waistline without your knowing it. If you are dieting, the recipes may help keep you on the right track so that someday you'll be able to enjoy all the other desserts in this book— without tipping the scale in the wrong direction!

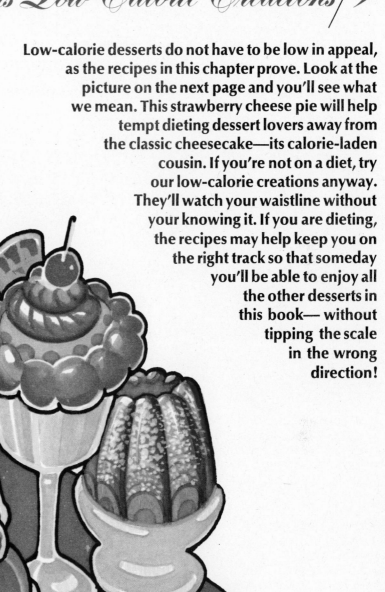

Both dieters and non-dieters will love Strawberry
Glazed Cheese Pie, a delicious dessert
that offers a great big bonus. Each serving
has only 177 calories! Recipe is in this chapter.

Frosted Devil's Angel Cake shows how to have your cake and diet, too! It's only 133 calories per serving. Recipe is in this chapter.

8-CALORIE CHOCOLATE KISSES

Bake at 275° for 20 minutes.
Makes 9 dozen kisses at 8 calories each.

    3 egg whites
    ½ teaspoon cream of tartar
    1 cup fine granulated sugar
    2 tablespoons unsweetened cocoa powder

1. Beat the egg whites in small bowl of electric mixer until foamy. Add cream of tartar; beat until soft peaks form. Gradually beat in sugar. Fold in cocoa 1 tablespoon at a time.
2. Use a measuring teaspoon to drop level spoonfuls of meringue mixture on nonstick cooky sheets.
3. Bake in a slow oven (275°) 20 minutes. Let cool slightly on sheets before removing. Store in a very dry place.

LOW-CALORIE NESSELRODE PIE

Makes 10 servings at 147 calories each.

    1 envelope unflavored gelatin
    ½ cup sugar
    ¼ teaspoon salt
    3 tablespoons cornstarch
    1¾ cups skim milk
    3 egg yolks, beaten
    3 egg whites, stiffly beaten
      Sugar substitute to equal ¾ cup sugar
    1 teaspoon vanilla
    2 teaspoons brandy or rum extract
    3 maraschino cherries, chopped
      Low-Calorie Graham Cracker Pie Shell
      (page 132)

1. Combine gelatin, sugar, salt and cornstarch in top of double boiler. Add skim milk slowly. Place over simmering water.
2. Cook, stirring constantly, until thickened. Blend half the hot mixture into the egg yolks in a small bowl. Stir back into remaining mixture. Cook 2 minutes.
3. Remove from heat; pour into a medium-size bowl; cool. Stir in sugar substitute, extracts and cherries. Chill over ice and water until mixture mounds slightly when spooned.
4. Fold in stiffly beaten egg whites until no streaks of white remain. Pour into pie shell. Refrigerate about 4 hours, or until set.

STRAWBERRY GLAZED CHEESE PIE

Makes 10 servings at 177 calories each.

      Graham-Cracker Crust (recipe follows)
    ½ cup water
    ½ cup instant nonfat dry milk (powder)
    ½ cup sugar
    4 eggs
    ¼ teaspoon salt
    1 tablespoon lemon juice
    1 teaspoon vanilla
    ¼ cup flour
    1 pound cottage cheese (any kind)
      Jeweled Fruit Glaze (recipe follows)

1. Prepare a 9-inch pie plate, using Graham-Cracker Crust.
2. Combine water, dry milk powder, sugar, eggs, salt, lemon juice, vanilla, flour and cottage cheese in container of an electric blender; whirl until smooth. (Or you may sieve cheese into a bowl, add remaining ingredients, then beat with a rotary beater until smooth.) Pour into prepared crust.
3. Bake in very slow oven (250°) for 1 hour. Turn oven off and leave pie in oven for 1 hour longer, then remove from oven; cool.
4. Top the cooled pie with Jeweled Fruit Glaze. Chill until glaze is set.

GRAHAM-CRACKER CRUST

Grease side and bottom of pan recommended in recipe with 1 tablespoon butter or margarine (or 2 tablespoons diet margarine). Sprinkle with ½ cup of graham-cracker crumbs; press firmly into place. Chill 1 hour, or until firm.

JEWELED FRUIT GLAZE

Wash and hull 1 pint of strawberries. Leave whole or cut in half lengthwise. Arrange on top of pie, cut side down. Blend 1 tablespoon cornstarch with 1 cup of water in a small saucepan. Cook over low heat, stirring constantly, until clear and thickened. Add enough liquid sweetener to equal ½ cup sugar. Stir in a few drops red food coloring. Cool slightly. Spoon over strawberries.
VARIATIONS: Canned waterpack pitted red cherries, frozen or fresh blueberries, or canned pineapple chunks may be glazed the same way.

27-CALORIE PROTEIN-RAISIN GEMS

Bake at 375° for 8 minutes.
Makes 5 dozen cookies at 27 calories each.

   ¾ **cup sifted all-purpose flour**
   ⅓ **cup sifted low-fat soy flour**
   ½ **teaspoon baking soda**
   ½ **teaspoon salt**
   ½ **cup (½ an 8-ounce container) diet margarine**
   5 **tablespoons firmly packed brown sugar**
      Sugar substitute to equal 8 tablespoons sugar
   1 **teaspoon vanilla**
   1 **egg**
   1 **cup raisins**

1. Sift flour, soy flour, baking soda and salt onto wax paper.
2. Beat diet margarine, brown sugar, sugar substitute, vanilla and egg until well blended.
3. Add sifted dry ingredients to margarine mixture; mix well. Stir in raisins.
4. Use a measuring teaspoon to drop level spoonfuls of cooky dough on nonstick cooky sheets.
5. Bake in a moderate oven (375°) 8 minutes. Cool on paper toweling.

FROSTED DEVIL'S ANGEL CAKE

Bake at 350° for 40 minutes.
Makes 16 servings at 133 calories each; 77 calories without Fudge Frosting.

   ¾ **cup sifted cake flour**
   ¼ **cup unsweetened cocoa powder**
   ½ **cup sugar**
  10 **egg whites (1¼ cups)**
   ¼ **teaspoon salt**
   1 **teaspoon cream of tartar**
   ½ **cup sugar**
   ½ **teaspoon vanilla**
  1½ **tablespoons liquid sugar substitute**
      Fudge Frosting (recipe follows)

1. Sift flour, cocoa and ½ cup of the sugar onto wax paper.
2. Beat the egg whites with the salt and cream of tartar in large bowl with electric mixer until very foamy and peaks are beginning to form. Gradually beat in remaining ½ cup sugar. Con-

tinue beating until stiff peaks form. Beat in vanilla and liquid sweetener.
3. Gently fold the flour mixture into the egg whites, a few tablespoons at a time. Turn into an ungreased 9-inch spring-form pan. Carefully cut through batter with a spatula to avoid air pockets.
4. Bake in moderate oven (350°) 40 minutes, or until surface of cake is dry and springs back when lightly pressed with fingertip. Invert cake in pan on wire rack until cold.
5. Carefully loosen cake from side of pan; remove side. Loosen from bottom of pan. Serve as is, or split into three layers; reassemble with Fudge Frosting between layers and on top of cake. Leave side unfrosted. Garnish with a twist of orange, if you wish.

FUDGE FROSTING

Makes enough to assemble Devil's Angel Food Cake or to frost top and sides of a two-layer cake. Adds 56 calories to each serving of a 16-serving cake.

   1 **package (two 1¼-ounce envelopes) low-calorie whipped topping mix**
  1½ **cups cold water**
   1 **teaspoon vanilla**
   1 **package instant chocolate pudding**
      Pinch salt
      Sugar substitute to equal ¼ cup sugar
   1 **teaspoon instant coffee**

Combine all ingredients in small bowl. Beat with electric mixer at high speed for 2 minutes.

BLUSHING PEAR SQUARE

Bake at 325° for 25 minutes.
Makes 12 servings at 104 calories each.

   ¾ **cup sifted cake flour**
   1 **teaspoon baking powder**
   ½ **teaspoon pumpkin-pie spice**
   ¼ **teaspoon salt**
   2 **eggs**
   ⅓ **cup granulated sugar**
   ¼ **cup firmly packed light brown sugar**
   ¼ **cup boiling water**
      Blushing Pears (recipe follows)

1. Sift cake flour, baking powder, pumpkin-pie spice and salt onto wax paper.
2. Separate eggs, placing whites in a medium-size bowl and yolks in a small bowl.
3. Beat egg whites until foamy-white and double in volume; beat in granulated sugar, 1 tablespoon at a time, until meringue forms soft peaks.
4. Beat egg yolks until fluffy-thick; beat in brown sugar, 1 tablespoon at a time. Stir in boiling water; beat vigorously 5 minutes, or until mixture forms soft peaks.
5. Fold egg-yolk mixture into egg-white mixture until no streaks of yellow remain; fold in flour mixture, one-fourth at a time. Pour batter into an ungreased baking pan, 9x9x2.
6. Bake in slow oven (325°) 25 minutes, or until top springs back when lightly pressed with fingertip. Cool completely in pan on a wire rack.
7. While cake cools, prepare Blushing Pears (recipe follows).
8. Loosen cake around edges with a knife; turn out, then turn right side up on a serving plate. Lift pears from syrup and arrange in a pattern on top of cake; spoon syrup evenly over all. Cut into 12 serving-size pieces.

BLUSHING PEARS: Pare 3 medium-size firm ripe pears; quarter and core. Place pears and ¾ cup low-calorie cranberry-juice cocktail in a medium-size skillet. Heat to boiling; lower heat; simmer, turning pears several times, 10 minutes, or until tender. Blend 1 tablespoon cornstarch and ¼ cup more cranberry-juice cocktail until smooth in a cup; stir into liquid in skillet. Cook, stirring constantly, until mixture thickens and bubbles 1 minute; remove from heat; cool.

STRAWBERRY BAVARIAN PIE

Makes 10 servings at 57 calories each.

  1 **cup evaporated skim milk**
  1 **package (⅝ ounce-2 envelopes) low-calorie, strawberry-flavor gelatin**
  1½ **cups boiling water**
     Pinch of salt
     Sugar substitute to equal ¼ cup sugar
     Meringue (Angel) Pie Shell (page 132)

1. Pour evaporated skim milk into ice cube tray or loaf pan. Chill in freezer until ice crystals begin to form around edges. Chill small bowl and beaters of electric mixer in refrigerator.
2. Dissolve both envelopes strawberry gelatin in boiling water; stir in salt and sugar substitute. Chill over ice and water until cool and syrupy.
3. Pour the chilled evaporated skim milk into the chilled bowl. Beat at high speed until stiff, about 8 to 10 minutes. Fold into gelatin mixture until no streaks of white remain. Turn into pie shell. Refrigerate the pie for about 3 hours, or until it is set.

LOW-CALORIE LEMON CHIFFON PIE

Makes 8 servings at 129 calories each or 10 servings at 103 calories each.

  1 **envelope unflavored gelatin**
  ½ **cup cold water**
  2 **eggs, separated**
  1 **tablespoon grated lemon rind**
  4 **tablespoons lemon juice**
     Pinch of salt
  ¼ **cup sugar**
     Sugar substitute to equal ⅓ cup sugar
  ⅓ **cup ice water**
  ⅓ **cup nonfat dry milk powder**
     Low-Calorie Graham Cracker Pie Shell (page 132)

1. Soften envelope of unflavored gelatin in the ½ cup cold water.
2. Combine egg yolks, lemon rind, 3 tablespoons of the lemon juice, salt and sugar in the top of a double boiler. Cook over boiling water, stirring constantly, until mixture is thickened, about 5 minutes.
3. Remove from heat; stir in softened gelatin and sugar substitute. Cool the mixture just until it reaches room temperature.
4. Beat egg whites until stiff peaks form (use a non-plastic bowl). Measure ice water, remaining 1 tablespoon of lemon juice and nonfat dry milk powder into small bowl of electric mixer. Beat at high speed until mixture is the consistency of stiffly whipped cream, about 8 to 10 minutes.
5. Fold the beaten egg whites and whipped nonfat dry milk into gelatin mixture; turn into pie shell. Refrigerate about 4 hours, or until set.

MERINGUE (ANGEL) PIE SHELL

Bake at 275° for 1 hour, turn off heat and leave in oven 30 minutes longer.
Makes 1 nine-inch pie shell. Total calories: 310.

2 egg whites
Pinch of salt
Pinch of cream of tartar
½ teaspoon vanilla
7 tablespoons sugar

1. Beat egg whites in small bowl with electric mixer until frothy; add salt and cream of tartar. Beat until stiff but not dry. Add vanilla. Beat in sugar, 1 tablespoon at a time. Continue beating until stiff peaks form.
2. Spread meringue on bottom and side of a 9-inch nonstick pie pan (or greased pie plate).
3. Bake in very slow oven (275°) 1 hour, or until crisp. Turn off heat; leave meringue shell in oven 30 minutes longer. Cool.

EASY LOW-CALORIE BANANA PIE

Makes 8 servings at 173 calories each or 10 servings at 138 calories each.

2 envelopes unflavored gelatin
½ cup boiling water
3½ cups skim milk
½ teaspoon ground cinnamon
1 package (3¾ ounces) vanilla instant pudding mix
1 ripe banana
Low-Calorie Graham Cracker Pie Shell (recipe follows)

1. Place gelatin in container of electric blender; add boiling water. Whirl at high speed, scraping sides of container several times, until gelatin is dissolved.
2. Add about 2 cups of the skim milk (do not overfill container); blend briefly. Pour about half of mixture into bowl; add remaining milk and cinnamon to mixture in container; blend briefly.
3. Add pudding mix to milk mixture in container; blend until smooth. Add to blended mixture in bowl; mix well. Refrigerate a few minutes until mixture thickens.
4. Slice banana into bottom of pie shell; fill with filling. Refrigerate for 3 hours or until set.

LOW-CALORIE GRAHAM CRACKER PIE SHELL

Bake at 400° for 5 minutes.
Makes 1 nine-inch pie shell.
Total calories: 524.

3 tablespoons soft diet margarine
1 cup packaged graham cracker crumbs

1. Blend margarine and crumbs thoroughly, using a fork. Press evenly onto the bottom and side of a 9-inch pie plate, covering all surfaces expect the rim.
2. Bake in hot oven (400°) 5 minutes. Cool before filling.

GLAZED FRUIT MERINGUES

Bake at 250° for 1 hour.
Makes 8 servings at 58 calories each.

2 egg whites
1 teaspoon lemon juice
⅓ cup sugar
1 teaspoon vanilla
2 teaspoons cornstarch
Dash of ground cardamom
1 can (1 pound) calories-reduced fruits for salad
Red food coloring

1. Line a large cooky sheet with brown paper; draw eight 3½-inch rounds, 2 inches apart, on paper. (A regular coffee cup makes a handy pattern.)
2. Beat egg whites with lemon juice until foamy-white and double in volume in a small bowl. Sprinkle in sugar, 1 tablespoon at a time, beating all the time until sugar completely dissolves and meringue stands in firm peaks; beat in vanilla.
3. Divide the meringue onto the eight circles, with spoon, building up edge so meringue will hold the filling when baked.
4. Bake in very slow oven (250°) 1 hour, or until delicately golden. Cool on cooky sheet 5 minutes; loosen carefully from paper with a spatula; place on wire racks to cool.
5. About an hour before serving, mix cornstarch and cardamon in a small saucepan. Drain syrup from fruits and blend into cornstarch mixture until smooth.
6. Cook, stirring constantly, until mixture thick-

ens and boils 3 minutes; remove from heat. Stir in a drop or two food coloring to tint rosy red; cool.

7. Halve any large pieces of fruit; arrange pieces in meringue shells. Brush fruits with tinted syrup to glaze lightly.

TANGY GINGERBREAD

Bake at 350° for 30 minutes.
Makes 12 servings at 104 calories each.

    1 cup sifted all-purpose flour
    ½ teaspoon baking soda
    ¼ teaspoon salt
    1 teaspoon ground cinnamon
    1½ teaspoons ground ginger
       Pinch ground cloves
    1 egg
    6 tablespoons firmly packed brown sugar
    ¼ cup molasses
    ½ cup soured skim milk*
    2 tablespoons butter or margarine, softened

1. Sift flour, baking soda, salt, cinnamon, ginger and cloves onto wax paper.
2. Beat egg with sugar and molasses until light. Add the soured skim milk, butter and flour mixture; beat until smooth. Turn into an 8-inch square nonstick baking pan.
3. Bake in a moderate oven (350°) 30 minutes, or until center springs back when lightly pressed.
*To make soured milk, place 2 teaspoons lemon juice or vinegar in a 1-cup measure. Add skim milk to ½-cup mark.

ORANGE "CREAM CHEESE" ICING

Makes enough to frost 2 layers.
Makes 16 servings at 37 calories each.

    6 ounces Neufchâtel cheese, softened
    1 teaspoon grated orange rind
    1 tablespoon orange juice
    ¼ cup 10X (confectioners') sugar
       Sugar substitute to equal ½ cup sugar

Combine cheese and orange rind and juice in small bowl. Beat with electric mixer until smooth. Add 10X sugar and sugar substitute; beat until the mixture is fluffy.

PEARS IN BURGUNDY

Makes 4 servings at 110 calories each (with sugar), 86 calories with sugar substitute.

    1 can (16 ounces) diet-pack pear halves
    ½ cup dry red wine
    ½ cup orange juice
    ½ teaspoon ground cinnamon
    ¼ teaspoon ground cloves
    ¼ teaspoon grated lemon or orange rind
    3 tablespoons sugar OR: Sugar substitute to equal 3 tablespoons of sugar

1. Drain pear juice into a small saucepan; add wine, orange juice, cinnamon, cloves, lemon or orange rind and sugar. Bring to boiling; lower heat. Simmer, uncovered, until liquid is reduced to half of original volume. Cool a few minutes.
2. Arrange pear halves in 4 stemmed glasses. Pour warm liquid over pears; chill before serving.

FRENCH FRUIT PIE

Makes 8 servings at 148 calories each.

       Low-Calorie Graham Cracker Pie Shell (page 132)
    ½ package low-calorie vanilla pudding and pie filling
    1 cup skim milk
    1 can (1 pound) calories-reduced cling peach slices
    1 can (8½ ounces) calories-reduced pineapple tidbits
    1 tablespoon cornstarch
    1 teaspoon orange extract

1. Prepare Low-Calorie Graham Cracker Pie Shell.
2. Prepare pudding mix with the 1 cup skim milk following label directions; refrigerate.
3. Drain liquids from peaches and pineapple into a cup, then blend into cornstarch until smooth in a small saucepan. Cook, stirring constantly, until glaze thickens and bubbles for about 1 minute. Stir in the orange extract; let mixture cool.
4. Spread chilled pudding in crumb shell. Arrange peaches and pineapple on top. Spoon glaze over fruits. Refrigerate until glaze is set.

MOLDED CHEESE SNOW WITH STRAWBERRIES

Makes 6 servings at 82 calories each.

1 container (12 ounces) pot cheese
⅓ cup skim milk
2 tablespoons dairy sour cream
1 teaspoon vanilla
 Sugar substitute to equal 2 tablespoons sugar
1 pint (2 cups) strawberries, washed, hulled and halved

1. Combine pot cheese and skim milk in an electric-blender container; cover. Beat until smooth; pour into a medium-size bowl. (If you do not have a blender, press cheese through a sieve into a medium-size bowl; stir in skim milk.)
2. Stir in sour cream, vanilla, sugar substitute.
3. Line 6 individual heart-shape or regular molds with cheesecloth large enough to hang over edge; pack cheese mixture into molds; fold cheesecloth over tops. Set molds in a pan for easy handling. Refrigerate at least 3 hours.
4. When ready to serve, fold back cheesecloth; invert molds onto serving plates; peel off cloth. Arrange strawberries around molds, placing a whole one on top, if you wish.

PINEAPPLE PUFF

Makes 8 servings at 113 calories each.

4 eggs, separated
1 can (1 pound, 4 ounces) juice packed crushed pineapple
 Granulated, liquid or tablet no-calorie sweetener to equal 8 tablespoons sugar
2 envelopes unflavored gelatin
¾ cup instant nonfat dry milk
¾ cup ice water

1. Prepare a 4-cup soufflé dish: Cut a strip of foil, 12 inches wide and long enough to go around dish with a 1-inch overlap; fold in half lengthwise. Wrap around dish to make a 2-inch stand-up collar; hold in place with a rubber band and a paper clip.
2. Beat egg yolks in the top of a double boiler; stir in pineapple and juice and your favorite no-calorie sweetener. Sprinkle gelatin over top; let stand several minutes to soften gelatin. Place top of double boiler over simmering water.
3. Cook, stirring constantly, 15 minutes, or until gelatin dissolves and mixture coats a spoon; pour into a large bowl.
4. Set bowl in a pan of ice and water; chill, stirring several times, just until as thick as unbeaten egg white.
5. While pineapple mixture chills, beat egg whites just until they form soft peaks in a medium-size bowl.
6. Sprinkle dry milk powder over ice water in a chilled medium-size bowl; beat with an electric beater at high speed until stiff.
7. Fold beaten egg whites, then whipped milk into gelatin mixture, keeping bowl over ice, until no streaks of white remain. Pour into prepared soufflé dish. Chill several hours, or until firm. Spoon into serving dishes; garnish each with a sprig of mint, if you wish.

HEAVENLY ANGEL CAKE

Bake at 350° for 40 minutes.
Makes 16 servings at 79 calories each.

1 cup sifted cake flour
1 cup sugar
10 egg whites (1¼ cups)
¼ teaspoon salt
1 teaspoon cream of tartar
½ teaspoon vanilla
1½ tablespoons liquid sugar substitute

1. Sift flour and ½ cup of the sugar onto wax paper.
2. Beat the egg whites with salt and cream of tartar in large bowl with electric mixer until very foamy and peaks begin to form. Gradually beat in the remaining ½ cup sugar. Continue beating until stiff peaks form. Beat in vanilla and liquid sugar substitute.
3. Gently fold the flour mixture into the egg whites, a few tablespoons at a time. Turn into an ungreased 9-inch spring-form pan. Carefully cut through batter with a spatula to avoid air pockets.
4. Bake in moderate oven (350°) 40 minutes, or until surface of cake is dry and center springs back when lightly pressed with fingertip. Invert cake in pan on wire rack until cold. Carefully loosen cake from side of pan; remove side.

21-CALORIE PEANUT BUTTER COOKIES

Bake at 375° for 8 minutes.
Makes 5 dozen cookies at 21 calories each.

⅔ cup sifted all-purpose flour
½ teaspoon baking soda
½ teaspoon baking powder
3 tablespoons butter or margarine, softened
4 tablespoons peanut butter
2 tablespoons firmly packed brown sugar
  Sugar substitute to equal 4 tablespoons of sugar
1 teaspoon vanilla
2 eggs, beaten

1. Sift flour, baking soda and baking powder onto wax paper.
2. Beat the butter or margarine, peanut butter, brown sugar and sugar substitute together. Add vanilla and eggs; beat until fluffy.
3. Add sifted dry ingredients to peanut butter mixture; mix well.
4. Use a measuring teaspoon to drop level spoonfuls of cooky dough on nonstick cooky sheets.
5. Bake in a moderate oven (375°) for 8 minutes. Cool on paper toweling.

CHOCOLATE-ALMOND ROLL

Bake at 400° for 8 minutes.
Makes 10 servings at 112 calories each.

½ cup sifted cake flour
¾ teaspoon baking powder
¼ teaspoon salt
3 eggs
½ cup granulated sugar
1 teaspoon almond extract
1 tablespoon 10X (confectioners') sugar
½ package low-calorie chocolate pudding and pie filling mix
1½ cups skim milk
2 tablespoons toasted slivered almonds

1. Lightly butter a 15x10x1-inch jelly-roll pan; line bottom with wax paper; butter paper.
2. Measure flour, baking powder and salt into sifter.
3. Beat eggs until foamy-light and double in volume in a large bowl; beat in granulated sugar, 1 tablespoon at a time, until mixture is thick; stir in almond extract.
4. Sift flour mixture over top, then fold in; pour into prepared pan.
5. Bake in hot oven (400°) 8 minutes, or until center springs back when lightly pressed with fingertip. Loosen cake around edges with a knife; invert onto a towel dusted with the 1 tablespoon 10X sugar; peel off wax paper. Trim crisp edges from cake. Starting at a short end, roll up cake, jelly-roll fashion; cool completely.
6. Prepare pudding mix with the 1½ cups skim milk, following label directions; chill.
7. Unroll cake carefully. Spread with all but ½ cup of the pudding; reroll. Place on serving plate; chill.
8. Just before serving, spread reserved ½ cup pudding in a ribbon over cake; sprinkle with almonds. Cut cake crosswise into 10 slices.

PUMPKIN SPICE CAKE

Bake at 325° for 1 hour.
Makes 16 servings at 160 calories each.

2¼ cups sifted cake flour
3 teaspoons baking powder
2 teaspoons pumpkin pie spice
½ teaspoon ground cinnamon
½ teaspoon butter-flavored salt
6 eggs, separated
⅔ cup diet margarine
1 cup canned pumpkin
¾ cup firmly packed brown sugar
  Sugar substitute to equal ⅔ cup sugar
½ teaspoon cream of tartar

1. Sift flour, baking powder, spice, cinnamon and salt onto wax paper.
2. Combine egg yolks, diet margarine, pumpkin, brown sugar and sugar substitute in a large mixing bowl; beat until smooth.
3. Add flour mixture gradually to egg-pumpkin mixture; after each addition, beat until blended.
4. Combine egg whites and cream of tartar in large bowl. Beat with electric mixer until stiff peaks form. Gently fold egg yolk batter into egg whites until just blended. Turn into a 10-inch nonstick tube or bundt pan.
5. Bake in slow oven (325°) 1 hour, or until top springs back when lightly pressed. Invert cake in pan on rack; cool. Carefully loosen from pan.

UPSIDE-DOWN APPLE CAKE

Bake at 350° for 35 minutes.
Makes 10 servings at 111 calories each.

> 1 cup sifted cake flour
> 1½ teaspoons baking powder
> Pinch salt
> 2 medium-size apples, pared and sliced
> 1 teaspoon lemon juice
> ½ cup firmly packed brown sugar
> ½ teaspoon ground cinnamon
> 2 eggs, separated
> Sugar substitute to equal ⅔ cup sugar
> ⅓ cup hot water
> 2 teaspoons vanilla

1. Sift flour, powder and salt onto wax paper.
2. Arrange sliced apples on bottom of an 8-inch square nonstick baking pan; sprinkle with lemon juice, 1 tablespoon of the brown sugar and cinnamon.
3. Beat egg yolks with the remaining brown sugar and sugar substitute; add hot water and vanilla. Beat until well-blended.
4. Add flour mixture to egg-yolk mixture; blend well. Beat egg whites until stiff; fold in. Spread batter over apples.
5. Bake in moderate oven (350°) 35 minutes, or until center springs back when lightly pressed with fingertip. Invert cake on serving plate; serve warm.

32-CALORIE APRICOT PINWHEELS

Bake at 375° for 12 minutes.
Makes 7 dozen cookies at 32 calories each.

> 1 cup dried apricots, finely chopped
> ½ cup boiling water
> 2½ cups sifted all-purpose flour
> ½ teaspoon baking powder
> 10 tablespoons butter or margarine, softened
> ¼ cup firmly packed brown sugar
> Sugar substitute to equal 4 tablespoons of sugar
> 6 tablespoons cold water

1. Combine apricots and boiling water in small bowl; allow to stand until most of water is absorbed. Drain.
2. Sift the flour and baking powder into bowl.

3. Beat butter or margarine, brown sugar, sugar substitute and water until well blended; add to flour mixture. Blend with a fork until the dough forms a ball.
4. Place dough on wax paper; flatten slightly. Wrap in the wax paper; chill in freezer 20 minutes.
5. Roll out dough on a floured surface to form 10x24-inch rectangle. Spread drained apricots over dough. Roll up dough from the longer side to form a 24-inch long roll; cut in half. Wrap each roll tightly in wax paper. Chill in refrigerator 3 hours or overnight.
6. Cut rolls into ⅜-inch-thick slices. Place on nonstick cooky sheets.
7. Bake in a moderate oven (375°) for 12 minutes. Cool on paper toweling.

23-CALORIE APPLESAUCE COOKIES

Bake at 375° for 15 minutes.
Makes 9 dozen cookies at 23 calories each.

> 1⅔ cups sifted all-purpose flour
> 1 teaspoon baking soda
> ½ teaspoon salt
> 2 teaspoons apple-pie spice
> 1 cup (8 ounces) diet margarine
> 5 tablespoons firmly packed brown sugar
> Sugar substitute to equal 6 tablespoons of sugar
> 1 teaspoon vanilla
> 1 egg
> 1 cup unsweetened applesauce
> ⅔ cup raisins
> 1 cup whole bran cereal

1. Sift flour, baking soda, salt and apple-pie spice onto wax paper.
2. Beat diet margarine, brown sugar, sugar substitute, vanilla and egg until blended (mixture will be rough and broken in texture due to the composition of the diet margarine).
3. Add sifted dry ingredients alternately with applesauce. Mix well after each addition. Stir in raisin and bran cereal.
4. Use in measuring teaspoon to drop level spoonfuls of cooky dough on nonstick cooky sheets.
5. Bake in a moderate oven (375°) 15 minutes, or until cookies are golden brown. Cool on paper toweling. Store in a covered container.

A traditional dessert takes on skinny dimensions
in this delicious version of Baked Apple Alaska. It has only
145 calories per serving. Recipe is in this chapter.

Calorie-shy fruit combines with light and
lovely meringues in Glazed Fruit Meringues,
a dessert with only 58 calories a serving.
The recipe is in this chapter.

BAKED APPLE ALASKA

Bake at 425° for 30 minutes, then 500° for 3 minutes.
Makes 10 servings at 145 calories each.

  5 apples, pared, cored and thinly sliced
  3 tablespoons granulated sugar
  2 teaspoons cornstarch
  ½ teaspoon ground cinnamon
    Pinch of salt
  1 quart vanilla ice milk
  3 egg whites
  ⅛ teaspoon cream of tartar
  ¼ cup 10X (confectioners') sugar

1. Arrange sliced apples in a 9-inch pie plate. Combine sugar, cornstarch, cinnamon and salt; sprinkle evenly over apples. Cover with foil.
2. Bake in hot oven (425°) 30 minutes, or until apples are just tender. Remove from oven; cool. Refrigerate. This may be done ahead.
3. At serving time, cover chilled apples with an even layer of ice milk. Place in freezer.
4. Beat egg whites and cream of tartar until frothy. Gradually add 10X sugar, a tablespoon at a time. Continue beating until mixture stands in peaks. Spread meringue over ice milk, being sure to bring it to the edge of the pie plate. Place pie plate in a roasting pan; surround with ice cubes to keep cold.
5. Bake in very hot oven (500°) 3 minutes, or until meringue is lightly browned. Remove from oven and ice; serve immediately.

CHOCOLATE SWIRL PIE

Makes 8 servings at 151 calories each.

  1 envelope (1 ounce) low-calorie chocolate pudding and pie filling
  1 envelope unflavored gelatin
    Pinch of salt
  2 cups skim milk
  1½ cups thawed, frozen non-dairy whipped topping
    Low-Calorie Graham Cracker Pie Shell (page 132)

1. Combine pudding mix, gelatin and salt in a medium-size saucepan. Add skim milk; stir until mixture is well blended.

2. Cook over medium heat, stirring constantly, until mixture thickens and bubbles. Remove from heat; cover surface with wax paper. Cool.
3. Remove wax paper; stir pudding until smooth. Swirl in whipped topping; turn into pie shell. Refrigerate about 3 hours, or until set.

ORANGE JEWEL PIE

Makes 8 servings at 113 calories each.

  1 package (⅝ ounce-2 envelopes) lemon-flavor, low-calorie gelatin
  2 cups boiling water
  1 cup cold water
  1 cup drained, calories-reduced mandarin orange sections (from a 10½-ounce can)
    Low-Calorie Graham Cracker Pie Shell (page 132)
  1 cup thawed, frozen non-dairy whipped topping

1. Combine gelatin and boiling water; stir until dissolved. Add cold water.
2. Chill over ice and water, stirring occasionally, until mixture mounds. Fold in orange sections. Carefully spoon into prepared pie shell.
3. Refrigerate about 3 hours or until firm. Spoon topping around edge before serving.

32-CALORIE COCONUT MACAROONS

Bake at 350° for 15 minutes.
Makes 3 dozen cookies at 32 calories each.

  2 egg whites
    Pinch of salt
    Pinch of cream of tartar
  1 can (7 ounces) shredded coconut (2 cups)
  2 tablespoons cake flour
  ¼ teaspoon baking powder

1. Beat the egg whites in small bowl of electric mixer until foamy. Add salt and cream of tartar; beat until stiff peaks form.
2. Combine coconut, cake flour and baking powder on wax paper. Fold into egg whites.
3. Use a measuring teaspoon to drop level spoonfuls on nonstick cooky sheets.
4. Bake in a moderate oven (350°) 15 minutes, or until edges of cookies are browned. Cool.

Pears in Burgundy are extra low in calories and extra high in appeal. The recipe is included in this chapter.

Index

ACKNOWLEDGMENTS

All photographs by George Nordhausen except:
Fred J. Maroon, 3.
Bill McGinn, 114-115.
Rudy Muller, 72-73, 74, 102-103, 104.
Gordon Smith, 40.

Illustrations by:
Tom Daly: 9, 33, 45, 49, 59, 83, 95, 101 and 125.
Gyo Fujikawa: 6, 7, 11, 12-13, 39, 42-43, 52, 64-65.

The editor gratefully acknowledges the use of the following recipes: Strawberry Vacherin, page 26, compliments Four Seasons Restaurant, New York; Tarte a L'Orange, page 76, compliments Lutece, New York; Abby's Fabulous Chocolate Cake, page 31, compliments Mrs. Morton Phillips; Walnut Pie, Glazed Apple Cheese Pie, page 68 and Cider Apple Pie, page 70, reprinted by Permission of G.P. Putnam's Sons from "The New York Times Heritage Cookbook" by Jean Hewitt. Copyright © 1972 By The New York Times Company.

The High Altitude Baking Chart on page 8, compliments of Swans Down.